A Sunset Book

cabins

and VACATION HOUSES

By the editors of Sunset books

LANE BOOKS · MENLO PARK, CALIFORNIA

Edited by Bob Thompson

Executive Editor, Sunset Books: David E. Clark

Eleventh Printing January 1973

CONTENTS

THE HOUSE ON THE COVER *is an elegant affair located on the shore of Puget Sound in Washington. It is full of ideas for bringing the interior into contact with the house site. A raised ceiling section has clerestory windows on all four sides to bring daylight into the living room. The water-facing windows have a deep overhang to cut afternoon glare, and a deck so the owners can be outside even on stormy days. There is no railing between the deck and the beach just a jump below. Pilings add flavor and protection to the site: Architects: Kirk, Wallace, McKinley, A.I.A., and Associates. This view is the correct one. The cover view is reversed for book design purposes.*

Introduction

Sunset has had a book about cabins and vacation houses for a great many years now. This is the third "new" book on the subject, and each of the preceding two appeared with many revisions. We've watched the idea of cabins grow and change over the years.

The ancient edition on the subject was veritably a handbook on wilderness building. It was all full of woodsy lore that would have done credit to Lewis or Clark, or one of the other earlier explorers.

The more recent edition had moved away from such information as how to build a log cabin from materials gathered on the site, and devoted itself more to ways to find sites that smacked of the wilderness, and yet would permit reasonably efficient modern building methods to be employed in the construction of a sound and attractive "second home."

It contained, for example, extensive information on searching out a desert cabin site through means of the Small Tract Act of 1938. It contained even more information on applying for and developing a·cabin site in one of California's National Forests.

But the West is getting more populous, especially in the three Pacific states. Neither of the above resources remains available in 1966. It comes down very nearly to a matter of a private real estate transaction these days, except for some remaining opportunities to "homestead" in the Rocky Mountain states.

Yet, if the romantic notion has had to fade just a bit, the practical considerations are much easier to face. The pressure to have vacation retreats has caused a great many people to think about the idea long and hard. As usual, the result has been more and better ideas about cabins, followed by more and better materials for building them, with more and better financing programs organized for the purpose.

People who used to be content with the dream now find it possible to have a retreat.

Their great numbers have made it possible to search out new areas. Nothing points to this trend more strongly than the yearly increase of ski communities in California's Sierra, in Washington's Cascades, in Utah's lofty Rockies.

Now Sunset's book about cabins devotes itself primarily to demonstrating how much diversity there is in the idea of a cabin, and how widely prices range, and what awesome scenery still awaits a new generation of cabin builders.

It is still all there. A harried Los Angeles lawyer can still expect to find a fine lakeshore cabin site in the San Bernardino Mountains, within Friday evening driving range. A San Francisco stockbroker can look forward to weekends of slowpoke tidepooling within minutes of his cabin door, which in turn need be little more than an hour from his city door. A Seattle aircraft engineer has wide opportunity to build a cabin on some navigable waterway off Puget Sound, and any Portland executive who skis has ample opportunity to build near his favorite slope.

Swap any two interests and places, and it's still possible to get a family together with just the kind of cabin it has been dreaming about.

For starters, one of the real pleasures is browsing through other peoples' ideas, to see how much good can be gotten from a deck, or ways to block the late afternoon sun.

That is what this book is for. A scrapbook of ideas often teaches more than construction blueprints at the beginning, as it shows what the architect means when he says a cabin ought to be a simple machine for living that provides shelter, warmth, shade, and facilities for cooking, eating, bathing, and sleeping... all without the frills that go well in a city place, but only reduce the majesty of the outdoors that caused the cabin to be wanted in the first place.

CUSTOM CABINS

Ski and Snow Country

The mountains of the West...Cascades, Sierra, Rockies, and their lesser offshoots...are full of cabins and vacation houses. Some are in National Forests. Most are in the ever-growing ski communities.

In some places, the urge is to blend into the backdrop. In others, it is fashionable to be obtrusive, with bright colors and unusual forms. However the finishing might go, the basic construction has to be rugged where snows mount up to depths of 10 feet most winters.

This section demonstrates that ruggedness can be found in A-frames, standard buildings, and even 60,000 gallon tanks borrowed from California's wine industry.

CONSTRUCTION: *Curved glue-laminated arches form rigid trusses with floor joists. Interior walls optional.*

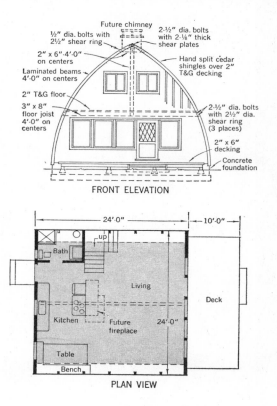

Future chimney
½" dia. bolts with 2½" shear ring
2-½" dia. bolts with 2-⅛" thick shear plates
2" x 6"·4'·0" on centers
Laminated beams 4'·0" on centers
Hand split cedar shingles over 2" T&G decking
2" T&G floor
3" x 8" floor joist 4'·0" on centers
2-½" dia. bolts with 2½" dia. shear ring (3 places)
2" x 6" decking
Concrete foundation

FRONT ELEVATION

24'·0" | 10'·0"
Bath
up
Living
Kitchen
Future fireplace
24'·0"
Deck
Table
Bench

PLAN VIEW

AT BRIGHTON *ski area, gothic arch form fits forest setting. Only 2 feet of 5-foot snow stayed on roof.*

The A-frame goes Gothic

ARCHITECT: RAYMOND A. JOHNSON

This refinement of the A-frame shares the economy of the A-frame in that its side walls are also its roof, but sacrifices less usable floor space to restricted headroom. (The second floor of this one, 20 by 24 feet, is only four feet narrower than the main floor.) The curved roof sheds most of the snow that falls on it. Roof and floor framing take the entire structural load, so walls are not needed for support and end walls can be finished in any material, including glass. Interior walls can be freely placed.

To cope with a short summer building season, the cabin was designed to go up fast. The glue-lam beams, a stock item for farm utility buildings, were pre-cut, drilled, and temporarily assembled before being trucked to the mountain site. On site, the arch trusses were assembled on the ground, then erected on the foundation; the center one was raised first, then plumbed and braced as a control point for others. As the 2-inch tongue-and-groove decking was nailed on, shingles were laid up concurrently to eliminate unnecessary scaffolding. Building was mainly a one-man project, with occasional help for the heavy parts.

LIVING ROOM WINDOWS *overlook creek, ski slopes. Roof masks fact that cabin is square. Exterior is cedar board-and-batten. Deck, a handy source of snowballs in winter, is favored summer sunning spot.*

Mountain cabin by a rushing creek

ARCHITECT: GEORGE T. ROCKRISE

CONCRETE BLOCK *foundation walls enclose 600 square feet of basement, which contains shop, firewood.*

Nestled in a mountain valley, at the bank of a rushing creek, this year-around vacation house is surrounded by exceptional natural beauty.

Its owner-architect made sure that seeing the rugged scenery is no trouble at all from anywhere inside the house. Each of the gables points to a fine scene. The unusual roof design permits the same kind of towering windows that A-frames have.

The other basic aim of the architect was to achieve the kind of spaciousness that will swallow up a herd of guests. He succeeded, in 1800 square feet. A by-product of this effort was the discovery of several money-saving techniques for construction.

Cost-cutting was not, however, at the expense of comfort, or practicality.

The downstairs bedrooms have a hall and doors for privacy. A bathroom on each floor is compartmented. The balcony-study is close enough to the windows to permit enjoyment of the living room windows and view. There is perimeter heating on both floors. The kitchen stove is electric. Hot water is abundant from an oil heater.

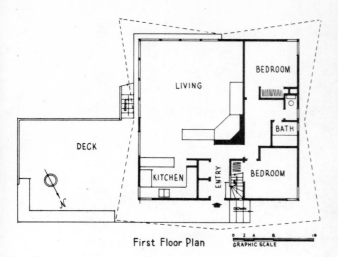

First Floor Plan

GRAPHIC SCALE
0 2 4 8 16

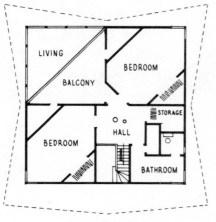

Second Floor Plan

FROM BALCONY, *which stretches diagonally across living room, forested slopes are in view.*

FLOOR PLANS *show how diagonals enhance utility of cabin. The gables take best advantage of the scenic beauty of the site. The balcony and upstairs bedrooms augment the views, maximize space.*

UPSTAIRS BEDROOMS *are identical. Ample closet space. No bedrooms side by side.*

BALCONY CREATES *two moods in living room—one snug, the other open to the awesome view outside.*

FINLIKE PROJECTIONS *in front (also around windows in back) serve as weather shields, reduce flow of cold air over glass. Doors could be added to fold across the fins when the cabin is not in use.*

A compact ski cabin

ARCHITECT: RON MOLEN

This compact mountain cabin in Park City, Utah, measures only 16 feet wide by 24 feet long, yet it seems unusually spacious. Partially combining roof with walls as it does, the modified A-frame design keeps materials and construction costs down while minimizing the foundation area. All of the materials were precut and prestained to make it even more of a money-saver. The "pulled-out" A-frame design permits greater utilization of the interior space than a standard A-frame does—and the squared-off top of the "A" adds to the uniqueness of the cabin's design.

On the main level there's a living-eating area, partly concealed kitchen, and bath. The upper level is a sleeping loft. Half of it is partitioned off to function as a private bedroom, and the other half opens to a two-story-high entry hall to give the cabin its spacious effect and provide daylight to both levels. The cabin accommodates seven without crowding—two sleep on the built-in couches on the main level, five more in the loft.

SPACIOUS ENTRY *has room for putting on, taking off, hanging outdoor gear; high windows are source of daylight.*

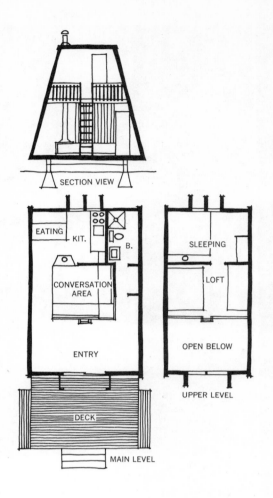

SECTION VIEW

EATING KIT.

B.

CONVERSATION AREA

ENTRY

DECK

MAIN LEVEL

SLEEPING

LOFT

OPEN BELOW

UPPER LEVEL

CONVENIENT STORAGE *for skis and poles is built into projecting "fins" on both sides of the entry.*

SLEEPING LOFT *is reached by permanent ladder from the entry. Compact beds are built into the floor.*

SUNKEN CONVERSATION AREA *(see plan) is out of traffic flow to eating area and kitchen around the corner.*

IN WINTER *the cabin appears to float above the snows drifted around it. The owners mounted a floodlight in the eaves outside the windows so they could watch snowstorms swirl through the night skies.*

With its unusual roof...

ARCHITECT: HENRIK BULL

The rewards of looking out through the tall corner windows of this cabin are a dramatic view and a sense of being perched high in a mountain lookout.

It demonstrates a point worth the notice of anyone dreaming about or planning a mountain cabin: There is no need to turn away from the scenery just to gain protection from the elements.

Basically, this cabin is a square box placed so that one corner juts from the slope. This corner, all glass, faces out over Squaw Valley near Lake Tahoe. It does face into some winter storms; yet it deflects winds as the prow of a ship deflects water.

The south-facing windows trap enough warmth from the winter sun to roughly compensate for the heat loss they allow during the night.

The diamond-shaped roof folds diagonally over the cabin, creating an illusion that the cabin is not square, and permitting an expansive sleeping loft. Beneath the sleeping loft and well back from the view windows is a snug, cave-like living area. A fireplace is its central point.

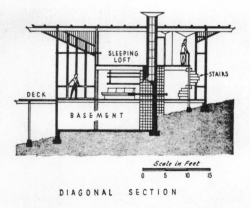

DIAGONAL SECTION

DIAGONAL BEAM *allows full headroom at center of loft, 4½ feet at sides. Basement with outside entrance provides storage for skis, houses forced-air furnace that augments fireplace.*

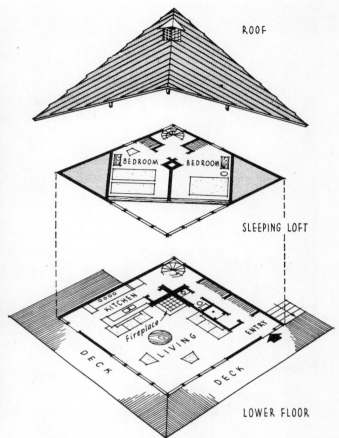

ROOF

BEDROOM   BEDROOM

SLEEPING LOFT

KITCHEN   Fireplace   LIVING   ENTRY   DECK   DECK

LOWER FLOOR

IN SUMMER, *cabin nestles down among surrounding trees. Deck expands its living space.*

COMPACT DESIGN *utilizes all of 576 square feet on main level, 400 square feet in loft.*

the feeling of a mountain lookout

Most visitors remark on the feeling of roominess in the cabin, a feeling created largely by the distinctly differing moods of the snuggery and the area next to the towering windows.

The cabin was built by its owner, who had little previous construction experience. The final result expresses his interest and architect Bull's in materials that fit into the changing moods (and disciplines) of the mountains.

The siding is of untreated redwood, chosen because it weathers at high altitudes to a rich rust color otherwise found in the most picturesque of chalets in the Swiss Alps. Doors and inside walls of other wood are painted a bright sky blue.

The ceiling is of alternating 2 by 3's and 2 by 2's nailed together. The pattern is pleasant, but the reason behind them is the need for a roof strong enough to support Sierra snows without cross beams. Cross beams would have been a serious inconvenience to all but tots in the sleeping loft.

All rough construction is in Douglas fir.

SNUG RETREAT *beneath sleeping loft floor is well-warmed by its efficient fireplace.*

HOUSE *is about eight feet above snow, for feeling of privacy, to free sleeping deck from night creatures.*

A mountain house designed to grow

ARCHITECTS: CAMPBELL & WONG

Many families outgrow their vacation houses after a few years. Adding on is not always the best answer; some houses just do not grow gracefully, and the site sometimes presents obstacles. But any such problems can be avoided if the plan is designed to expand as was done here.

Using a hexagon plan the designer made full use of windows at the two ends and lets the other wall "enfold or protect" the inside, without hampering the view that surrounds the cabin site.

Ample deck space is evident in all stages.

Stage 1 was built with a temporary kitchen and living area, two bedrooms and bath. No closets were put into the basic unit, instead pegs and racks being used in order to make later transformation easier.

When stage 2 is complete the living area will become two bedrooms and the kitchen will be converted into a hallway between units 1 and 2. Stage 2 will consist of living room, dining room and kitchen.

Two more bedrooms plus a lounge area and bath will be added in the stage 3 unit. Fireplaces are planned for all three units, the largest of which is a masonry fireplace in stage 2.

The simple sketch at the right shows how this mountain house will progress and how the first unit will be modified.

KITCHEN NOW *along inside wall of living area. Later this will become the hall leading to second unit.*

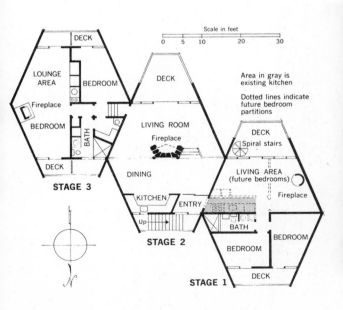

Scale in feet
0   5   10   20   30

DECK

LOUNGE AREA   BEDROOM

Fireplace

BEDROOM   BATH

DECK

STAGE 3

N

DECK

LIVING ROOM

Fireplace

DINING

KITCHEN   ENTRY

Up

STAGE 2

Area in gray is existing kitchen

Dotted lines indicate future bedroom partitions

DECK   Spiral stairs

LIVING AREA (future bedrooms)   Fireplace

BATH

BEDROOM   BEDROOM

DECK

STAGE 1

ONE DECK *is off living room (stage 1) with circular stairs to ground below. Later this will be bedrooms.*

SNOWFLAKE DESIGN *allows maximum south exposure. Snow easy to push off deck between rail supports.*

ENTRY BRIDGE *is above highest winter snow levels, ends in sheltered storage space for ski gear.*

"Snowflake" house with a bridge

ARCHITECTS: VOLKMANN & STOCKWELL

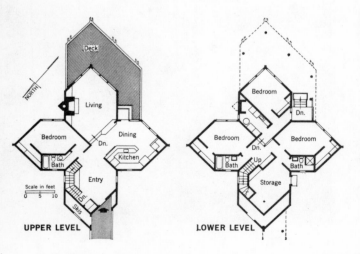

This luxurious mountain house lacks none of the comforts of any city home while it reaps the rewards of its location high in California's Sierra Nevadas.

It is on two levels. The main living areas are grouped on the upper level to take advantage of the view and to be above the deep snow in winter.

The engaging snowflake design helps windows in the living room and dining-kitchen area face south to get the most warmth from a low winter sun. The deck looks south for the same reason.

The approach to the house is along a raised bridge that runs from the parking area (no carport) to the front door.

By the front door is a bench where ski boots can be removed. Opposite is a closet which holds cleaning equipment and trash cans as well as skis and the other outdoor gear. The entry has an easily-mopped stone floor.

When the house is unoccupied, the thermostat is kept at 40° to avoid frost or mildew damage to the utilities or furnishings.

LIVING ROOM LOWER *than rest of main floor by two steps to gain vertical space. Ceiling throughout is edge-laid 2 by 4's. All colors chosen to match rocks, plants, trees native to the beauteous site.*

DINING ROOM, *kitchen share one point of the snow-flake. All view windows purposely kept unshaded, draped.*

TRIANGULAR BATTENS *on master bedroom inside wall match the exterior siding of the house.*

THRUSTING, BOAT-LIKE FORM *accentuated by built-up ridge beam has roots in Scandinavian tradition. Glass wall allows view of ski slopes from either living room or balcony bedrooms on rear side of house.*

Mountain cabin with a nod

ARCHITECT: HENRIK BULL

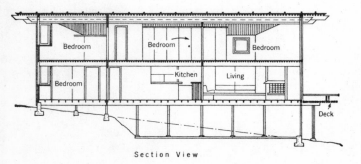

CROSS-SECTION *is in perspective with photo above.*

This year-around vacation house has room for members of several generations of the owning family. The owners wanted a retreat for themselves and their friends, and a place for their sons and their families to entertain.

Costs were to be kept low on a sloping site faced toward ski slopes to the southwest. The architecture was to express the Scandinavian ancestry of the family.

The architect designed a house that is at once a shelter from and a vantage point to the outdoors, no matter whether a storm rages across the mountain slopes, or the air is sparkling clear above the ski runs.

By choice, the cabin faces directly into the afternoon sun, and faces that way with a large glass wall. The owners reasoned that it was a part-time house, and that they would be outdoors most of the time the sun shone anyway. Windows open low on the sun side and high on the shadow side, permitting a ventilation pattern that avoids

ENTRY IS CLOSED *ante-chamber, to prevent heat loss. Ski gear is stored in it. Floor is covered with fibre mats.*

LIVING ROOM *soars two stories next to glass wall, but offers snug retreat by fireplace under balcony.*

to Scandinavia

any significant heat build-up except when the house is closed tight. Also, the sun sinks beyond the high Sierra mountain rim to the west fairly early.

The soaring two-story living room with its attendant mountain view demands a refuge of cozy seclusion. The architect provided one, a hearthside sitting area tucked under the balcony with its two dormitory bedrooms.

The master and guest bedrooms are more private than the dormitories. They are at the rear of the house, the master on the lower floor and the guest bedroom upstairs.

The house is raised well above its sloping site so the entry is above the heaviest of snows, which reach as high as the level of the deck.

The lower section of the glass wall is curtained for night-time privacy from a section of road which runs along below the house. (The curtains are visible at the end panel of glass next to the entry.)

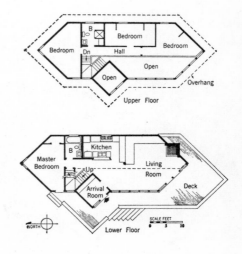

FLOOR PLAN *shows prow-like end walls clearly.*

TWO-STORY WINDOWS *open onto deck overlooking the lake. They provide light for living area, dormitory. Drapes conserve heat in winter. Small ventilation panels left and right of the door.*

BIG PLYWOOD PANELS *give air of snug solidness to the cabin. Cutback eaves lessen snow load on roof.*

There's room

ARCHITECT: JACK SIDENER

A dozen or so people can happily share this small cabin, and often do.

The architect designed it for extensive use in both summer and winter. A large central fireplace provides heat and an assurance of shelter, while the two-story end wall of the living room, with its high wall of glass, gives an effect of space and openness.

A dormitory provides expandable sleeping accommodations.

A long counter in the kitchen facilitates serving large groups, while the pullman kitchen is large enough for a chef, under-chef, and saucier all to work together.

The utility core-hallway holds a second toilet and lavatory and is also equipped with a washer and dryer.

To simplify construction, the architect used as exterior sheathing 4 by 8-foot plywood panels treated with wood

LOWER FLOOR *divides into living, eating, utility areas. Upper floor is entirely for sleeping.*

MASSIVE FIREPLACE, *of stone from the site, with its centilievered hearth, is winter gathering place.*

for a crowd in this small cabin

preservative then coated with plasticized varnish. These panels are secured in the post-and-beam framework by a system of 1 by 2's.

The interior walls and partitions are finished in V-grooved cedar lap siding, smooth side out in some rooms, rough, re-sawn side out in others.

The roofing is V-groove aluminum over a layer of 1-inch rigid insulation. Inside, the surface is tongue-and-groove. The eaves were cut back flush with the walls to prevent ice formation and layer-by-layer snow packing.

The main source of heat is a forced-air furnace, but the big fireplace has air-circulating tubes, with a fan built in, as a source of supplementary heat.

The site, overlooking Lake Tahoe in California, had several good trees and a natural ground cover. Added native plants help control erosion and cut down on dust.

LARGE KITCHEN *is next to utility area with its washer-dryer, and supply of firewood below stairs.*

CABIN RESTS ON PLATFORM, *its window wall faced to the view, its entry on the lee side during most storms. The redwood wine tank is thick enough to provide adequate insulation for winter use.*

Cabin-in-the-round...built from a wine tank

ARCHITECT: HENRIK BULL

The owner wanted a small vacation house that would not be boxy.

The architect proposed the round form as a solution, the redwood tank because the tank manufacturer was the only specialist equipped to work wood in curved forms.

The 60,000-gallon wine tank is a partial pre-fab in that the walls and roof are factory made. The manufacturer also did such mill work as window and door framing on the tank itself.

The architect planned the interior so the contractor could build in straight lines, with a maximum of right-angle intersections, for greatest efficiency.

The general contractor's crew erected the tank on a platform that also serves as the sub-floor and the deck. The tank is 26 feet in diameter, 16 feet high at the eaves, 19 feet high at the roof peak. Cost for the shell, erected, was about $4 per square foot of floor space. This amounted to between 25 and 33 per cent of the total investment.

What is it like to live in a 60,000-gallon wine tank? The pictures suggest some of the spaciousness and variety the round form gives to a small cabin. Although the cabin was designed mainly as a summer retreat in the Lake Tahoe, California, region, the 2⅝-inch thick tongue-and-groove walls insulate adequately for part-time winter use, even with the large glass area that faces the view. (Also, there is insulation beneath the floor.)

PEELED POST *is central roof support. Stairs lead from living area to sleeping balcony.*

BALCONY BEDROOM *privacy is enhanced by plywood panels set in rail. Wall (left) hides stair.*

SEE-THROUGH *connects snug kitchen with living room. Sink-refrigerator-stove are a single unit.*

DRAMATIC OPENNESS *combines with under-balcony snugness in living room. Windows open at bottom.*

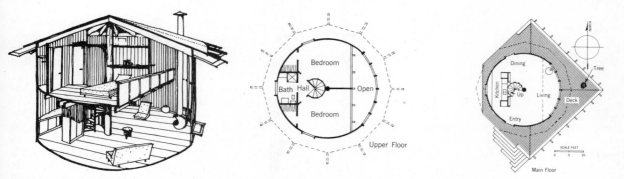

CUTAWAY SHOWS *interior relationship of rooms. Cabin has about 1,000 square feet of living space.*

BOAT STORAGE *area is under the deck. Timbers are extra heavy scale to support possible 18-foot snow load.*

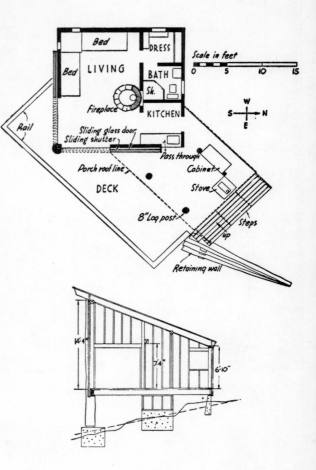

ELEVATION *shows how the foundation is set on slope.*

Mountain cabin with a view

ARCHITECTS: RUTH GERTH-GEORGE KOSMAK

BEDS SWING *out to be made. Circle around fireplace is volcanic stone. Back and sides are of firebrick.*

This cabin goes beyond merely carving shelter from the wilderness. The owners began by camping on every part of their site, learning it first hand. In this way they were able to save the best spot instead of building on top of it.

When the owners decided they were ready to build they called in professional help. The designers first asked the owners what they wanted of California's High Sierra (where their site was located). The answer: simply to be in it. So every view which could be seen from the cabin was worked out in the planning.

The sun was treated as both friend and enemy. Morning eastern sunlight may come in through an open wall to warm the cabin and wake sleepers, but by noon it is high enough that the deck's deep overhang shuts out bright overhead rays.

There was no strain to seek unusual building materials which would be used for their sake alone. Consequently the result is a mountain cabin that fits the owners as well as it fits the site.

THE OPEN *deck flooring drains water. Rail posts come up through the deck from the foundation below.*

PUP-TENT *shape was easy to frame. All uprights were cut from trees on the site. Cabin sleeps six.*

One-room triangular frame cabin

ARCHITECT: MRS. JOHN PRECHEK

Overlooking Lake Cavanaugh in western Washington, this cabin lies at the end of a narrow mountain road. It had to be built much in the way that all cabins used to be built, using local materials wherever possible, adapted to a shape that could be completely fabricated on the site.

Heavy timbers were cut on the property, so there couldn't be too many of them and they couldn't be too heavy. Shakes were hand split by workmen who lived nearby. A minimum of finished lumber was hauled in.

The cabin is both compact and efficient, and can sleep six. It can be closed by canvas which rolls down or by plastic screen shutters. With the canvas rolled up, the cabin opens wide on the deck.

The right side of the cabin is for cooking and dining; the left side for sleeping. In between is a fireplace made of an oil drum cut in two, with sand in the bottom.

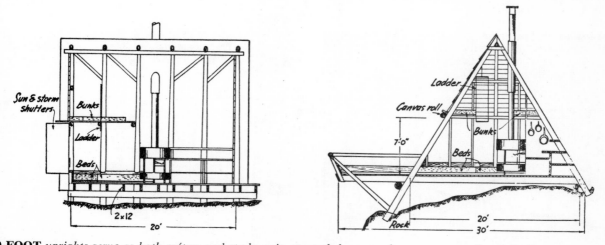

20-FOOT *uprights serve as both rafters and studs, gain strength by mutual support at roof's peak. 16-foot ceiling makes room for two beds placed high. End elevation: pyramidal shape gives broad base on hill.*

CABIN'S EXTERIOR *is brightened by burnt-orange ply-wood panels, black beams, natural redwood at the corners.*

SCREEN *of 2 by 4's separates living room from dining room. Perforated wallboard panels close off bedrooms.*

This mountain cabin sleeps 16

ARCHITECT: HENRIK BULL

This four-bedroom cabin has some good ideas for two or more families who plan a joint venture into cabin owner-ship. The 1675-square-foot floor plan presents a roomy cabin that sleeps 16 people (two double bunks in each bedroom) without infringing on the living areas.

The plan is based on a 4-foot module for economy of construction and maximum use of sheet materials. The floor and ceiling are of 1⅛-inch plywood, supported by a grid framework of 2 by 4's and 4 by 4's on 4-foot centers. The flat roof eliminates the complicated connections and expensive construction techniques found with gable or

shed roofs. The fireplace is economically constructed of concrete block, with the base extending below the floor.

The split-level design makes the floor plan work with-out requiring a space-wasting central hall. The front view wall is of double-post construction, giving a greater feel-ing of shelter as well as providing extra storage below the fixed glass.

The entry room between the deck and the living room provides storage space for ski boots and wet clothes, while cutting heat loss (that would result from a direct entry) and easing maintenance.

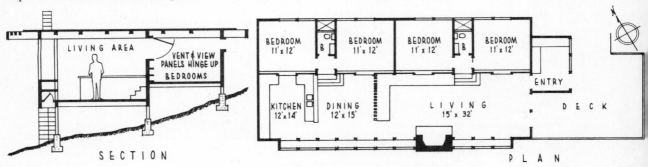

SECTION *shows how bedrooms, living room share view.*

PLAN *shows separation of living room and sleeping areas.*

CABIN'S INTERIOR *has soft warm colors. The walls and built-ins are of waxed clear western red cedar.*

A cabin of timber and river stone

ARCHITECT: ALAN LIDDLE

Few pre-cut materials went into the cabin which the owner designed and built near Mount Rainier in Washington.

From a deserted sawmill, he stripped off weather-silvered boards to use on the cabin ceiling. He took rough logs for the beams and split his cedar shakes from other logs on the land.

The stones came from the nearby Nisqually River. To build a wall that would be esthetically pleasing each stone was set with its length in a horizontal position, using stones with long, thin proportions. Variety was achieved by using different colors, textures and shapes. Unity was achieved by avoiding peculiar shapes and colors. Also, the owner tried not to place too many like stones together, and he didn't use small stones which would have given a fussy appearance.

The maximum size of the stones used was, of course, determined by one man's lifting capacity.

STONE WALLS *have natural insulating properties that make a cabin warmer in winter and cooler in summer.*

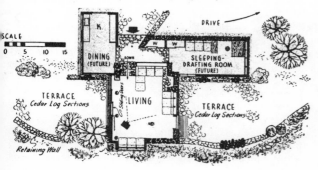

WOODED VALLEYS, *pine covered hills and sky above San Bernardino mountains are three walls of this interesting cabin. Ceiling follows pitched roof and the glass disappears into the ceiling without interruption.*

How about glass walls in a

ARCHITECT: LUCILLE BRYANT RAPORT

Most people could probably think of ten reasons why not to have glass walls in a mountain cabin. The designers and the owners could probably think of at least that many reasons why they feel glass walls are a good idea.

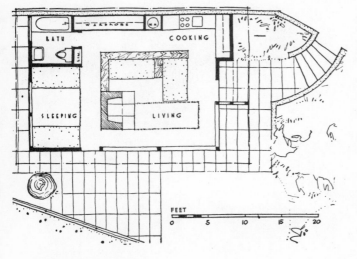

OVERHANGING *eaves project enough to prevent glare at standing height yet permit full view of mountains.*

This cabin was built as a guest house for a larger all-year home. The owners lived in it with great comfort while they waited for the completion of their larger house, located just up the slope overlooking the dam at Lake Arrowhead, California.

The architect likes the way the glass disappears into the roof, opening even the peak of the cabin to trees and sky. The structural engineer (Gordon deSwarte) likes the honest open use of the steel tie rods which serve both as curtain rods and as the lower chord of the roof truss.

The owners enjoy the free feeling of the mountains. They like the radiant heat from the warm floor panel and the ease of housekeeping regardless of the number of guests entertained.

How does it perform in the snow? Aren't the glass walls cold? Won't glass be broken by tree limbs in storms? How about snow against glass? What about vandals?

The glass traps the heat of the winter sun and keeps the cabin warm regardless of outside temperatures. At night and when there is no sun, drawn curtains help intercept loss of heat to cold glass.

Floor warmed by hot water, in wrought iron pipes in concrete slab, and heat-circulating fireplace are more than sufficient for the coldest days.

To protect glass from heavy drifts of snow, portable shutters can be hooked over the walls. Generally these are not needed for when the snow slides off the roof it is

LOW COUNTER *separates living and kitchen areas. Interior walls are combed plywood; ceiling is fiberboard.*

INTERIOR *is really one large room but curtains can be drawn to divide the living and sleeping areas.*

mountain cabin?

carried by its own weight out and away from the house. Also, the chimney is set at an angle to keep snow from piling up behind it.

The shutters protect the glass from tree limbs or possible damage by vandals whenever the house may be unoccupied for any length of time.

Forgetting cabin requirements for a moment, the application of design to a small house in the country offers several features of special interest.

The arrangement of space is flexible. One room is not unusual in a vacation house. But flexible arrangements in this 525-square-foot area is not obtained in the usual manner by scattering beds, tables and kitchen equipment along the walls of the room.

The fireplace and built-in counter give definite control of living, utility and sleeping space without lessening the spaciousness of the room.

The bedroom behind the fireplace is private, separated from the living quarters by curtains.

All of the kitchen equipment is lined up against the rear concrete wall of the house. The rear wall also stands as a retaining wall against the slope of the site.

To provide privacy when there are several guests, curtains are drawn between different sections.

All plumbing vents have been taken up between the roof rafters to the ridge. They are concealed by horizontal louvers running the length of the roof.

BRICK FIREPLACE *set around heat-circulating form. Beds slide to living room to be daytime couches.*

CUSTOM CABINS

Countryside & Lakeshore

On its lofty peaks, and at its ocean shore, the West offers rugged and brooding weather. Between, it is one of the most hospitable of the earth's inhabited climes.

Lakes, rivers, and streams full of fish are the primary goals of most vacation home and cabin builders. But still meadows and silent deserts are there, too, for the sturdy souls who enjoy the contemplations solitude can bring.

The gentleness of the climate gives free rein to architects and builders, and yet it is in such regions that the plainest buildings seem to be most numerous. The most frequent goal is a simple retreat that can be reached very soon after work ends Friday afternoon.

EXTENSIVE *use of glass makes house seem larger. Drapes give privacy if living area is used for sleeping.*

729-square foot vacation house

ARCHITECT: JACK HERMANN

A vacation house does not have to be very large to be quite usable, especially if it is not many hours' drive from the owners' home.

This one is only 27 feet square, but that is plenty of room for the architect and his family. Contained in the relatively small space are two bedrooms, bath, living-dining area, and kitchen. What's more it is only 25 miles from their Kentfield, California, home.

HEAT *is provided by a metal fireplace and a wall heater located in the center of the house (see above).*

ON WARM *summer days glass doors are opened and meals are carried from kitchen to outdoor sitting area.*

THE CABIN *stands just below a knoll in native trees, and has a view of Drake's Bay. It is up off ground and partly cantilevered beyond supports to discourage termites and mice. Deck has combination rail-seating.*

Small but spacious weekend retreat

ARCHITECT: IGOR SAZEVICH

This retreat for weekends and vacations in Inverness Ridge in California, contains only 750 square feet of interior space, yet it seems much larger. The owner-architect Igor Sazevich utilized some of the devices frequently employed to create both real and illusory space.

The living room is only 14 by 16 feet, but it is three feet below the level of the other rooms and gains extra vertical space by virtue of its higher ceiling. Tall glass windows across the end of the room emphasize the ceiling height, and a floor-level deck beyond seems to extend the room out into the trees.

A window-seat bay (at upper right in the plan) makes the room appear wider, and provides built-in seating without diminishing the floor space.

The kitchen and dining areas are open to the living room and share the same effect of space.

To free wall space in the bedrooms, the closets are located in the hall where they also function as a divider for the kitchen-dining areas. Expandable wall racks in the bedrooms hold everyday garments.

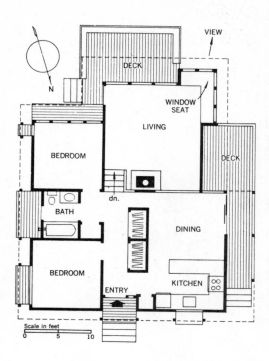

BEDROOMS *are of equal size (see plan); this one offers the same marine view as the living room and deck.*

ON WARM DAYS *or after a trip down to the beach, the family prefers to use this handy outdoor shower.*

COOKING-DINING *area is on upper level. Ceiling is grooved plywood; walls are plasterboard; floors are cork.*

GLASS-WALLED BEDROOM *overlooks a fine view of Puget Sound. Sleeping deck is at left, carport behind.*

A generous deck is all around

ARCHITECTS: TROGDON-SMITH

SOUTH-FACING BEDROOM *opens onto deck by glass door. Small window at left ventilates when door is closed.*

The natural beauty of a vacation house site is not always preserved as well as it was in this case.

Instead of clearing away the surrounding low brush, the architectural firm simply raised the house floor level about 30 inches to overlook it, and left the visible portions of the site virtually undisturbed.

The architects then brought the site into close contact with the house by means of a generous, covered perimeter deck, which also greatly expands the 650 square feet enclosed in the rectangular house.

The deck provides outdoor sitting and walking areas in the sometimes damp climate of Washington's San Juan Islands. It also eases the chores of window washing.

The sheltering deck roof extends seven feet beyond the house walls, a great eyeshade on sunny days as well as outdoor protection on the rainy ones.

DECK ROOF SUPPORTS *are paired 2 by 4's secured on either side of 2 by 6-inch vertical supports. The horizontal pieces pierce the walls, extend into rooms, as photo of living room (below) demonstrates.*

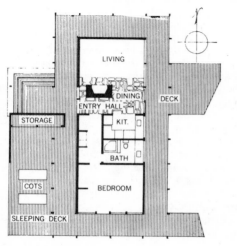

COVERED ENTRY *is a boon in any wet climate. Living room wall (see plan) was made windowless for privacy.*

VIEW FROM LIVING ROOM *is over water. Floor is slate. Kitchen is through the door in background.*

WIDE ROOF OVERHANG *cools the house on warm summer days in the Round Valley area of California's Eel River basin. The major glass areas face east to minimize glare. A skylight balances light.*

Wilderness retreat...the "wickiup"

ARCHITECT: IGOR SAZEVICH

FROM BACK SIDE, *the skylight at the crown of the roof is plainly visible. Bedrooms are on this side of the house.*

Its owners refer to their wilderness retreat as the "wicki-up." The design does suggest the shape of an Indian hut, but the construction is not at all casual.

This is essentially an 18-sided structure with a 52-foot diameter and a tentlike roof.

Half is used for a living-dining room. The remainder the architect designed for three bedrooms, three baths, and a kitchen area, as the floor plan shows.

The roof is supported on 20 wood columns cut on the property, and by a central chimney shaft of concrete. The exterior walls are in effect curtain walls, having no support function in the structure.

At the roof peak, a wire glass skylight around the flue opens the center of the structure to daylight, and is a fireproof spark-catcher into the bargain. A wire mesh on the flue minimizes flying embers in the air.

The exterior wood surfaces were left untreated to weather naturally. The roof is cedar shakes over 3 by 6-inch cedar sheathing. The walls are redwood. The supporting columns are peeled poles of Douglas fir.

TWENTY FEET FROM FLOOR *to roof peak. Fireplace central shaft is 38 inches in diameter. Roof beams are 6 by 14's. The floors are of polished redwood burls (collected by the owner) set over a concrete slab.*

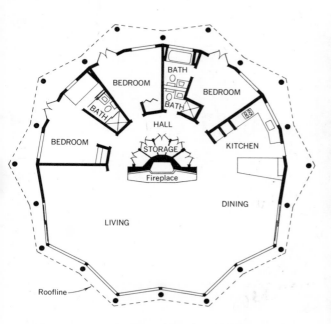

BEDROOM CEILINGS *are brought down to conventional height. Main storage areas back on fireplace.*

WOOD ROUNDS *are the patio floor, set flush with the main slab. Columns on piers to avoid rot, termites.*

FROM SLOPE BELOW, *prow shape of house is visible. Deck at floor level creates large usable area outdoors.*

OAKS SHADE DECK, *with its long view across lagoon to open sea. Trees are good as wind breaks, too.*

"A sort of tent"...it's a weekend

ARCHITECTS: MARQUIS & STOLLER

Section View

SCALE FEET
0   5   10   15

KITCHEN, INGLENOOK *tuck under sleeping balcony to help create cozy sense in a one-room house.*

The architects of this cabin started out with the premise that a one-room cabin can be as interesting as a more elaborate structure.

The owners, a family with four young children, wanted a small weekend house, a "sort of a tent," simple and natural to fit into a site on a wooded slope that overlooks the California coastline from Bolinas Lagoon as far south as (on the clearest of days) San Francisco.

The cabin is essentially one large room. A two-story high living room takes up more than half of the interior volume. A balcony sleeping area opens off it. Recessed below the balcony are the kitchen and an inglenook—a fireside retreat from the openness of the main area which, as its name indicates, is taken from the Scots. It is not in-

KITCHEN OPENS *freely into main living area.*
Door to right of kitchen is lower of two entries.

TENT-LIKE SWEEP *of roof makes living room open.*
Window seat designed to double as guest beds.

escape for the family

appropriate to compare this region of the California coast
to some of the loch country of Scotland, and it is not inappropriate for a cabin owner to want an inglenook.

Bath and storage are behind these spaces.

The house gains in interest from its hexagonal shape
and its steeply pitched roof. The three sides around the
living room are of glass, so this room seems open to the
deck that wraps around it. The deck in turn leads the eye
out to trees and beyond to the view over the water.

In contrast, the smaller spaces, on the closed three
sides, seem more intimate and sheltered. The lower-floor
spaces share the long view, but the sleeping balcony has
only the close-up view, through two-story glass, of the
surrounding woods.

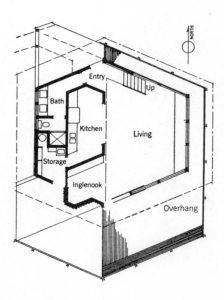

IN CENTER SECTION *you look through glass wall to living room and balcony bedroom above it. Porch at right.*

TOWER-LIKE *design was essential if house was to fit into the vertical space between these tall redwoods.*

A two-story room facing into a

INTIMATE AREA *by the metal hood fireplace is two steps below the level shown in photograph on page 41.*

This tall two-story room was designed to face into a tapestry of trees.

It could be called a hiding place cabin, located away from city life in the Santa Cruz Mountains in California. It is small enough for one person to feel comfortable, yet large enough for parties.

One observer noted "at first glance this house looks like the house of the three bears, an absurd fairy tale hut built by children. The materials are casual—intentionally unslick as if the architect felt that polished expensive details were not appropriate to a carefree house. The angled roofs, pipe chimney, and little window panes all express this seeming simplicity."

This is, obviously, not a cabin everyone would like. Some would think the casual appearance to be contrived or would argue that the interior stairway takes up too much of the center space in the house. Others are likely to consider the stair a novel part of the furnishings.

In designing the house the architects discarded formality and rules. The only entry is through the kitchen.

THE FLOOR LEVELS *in this cabin suddenly become benches: the window seat at left is an extension of the kitchen and the entry floor level. Sturdy stairway was built entirely free of walls, kitchen tucked in behind.*

tapestry of trees

The windows in no way balance one another. All rooms open into each other to give a feeling of openness rather than one of privacy.

The open stair makes of its lower landing an old fashioned window seat and of its upper landing a balcony bedroom. You walk across a bridge to get to the bathroom. The kitchen is tucked behind the stairs on lower level.

Steps are an important detail in the cabin's design. The main stairway sets the theme which is carried out by the second floor "bridge." A bench doubles as a step between the window-seat landing and the main level floor. The fireplace is located in a conversation well two steps below the main floor level.

At the rear of the cabin is a covered porch that is screened on three sides.

The size of the cabin is 567 square feet (excluding the porch).

Architects for this cabin were Charles W. Moore, Donlyn Lyndon, William Turnbull, Richard Whitaker, Warren C. Fuller, Associates.

UPPER LEVEL

Bath

Dn

Bedroom

MAIN LEVEL

Screened Porch

Living

Up

Kitchen

SCALE FEET
0   5   10

THE LARGE *deck was laid parquet style in 3-foot squares. 15-inch-high seat rail is of 2 by 8-inch boards.*

The deck is bigger than the cabin

FROM INSIDE *the cabin, the view is out across the deck and bay to green hills and the Olympic Mountains.*

This small summer cabin boasts more deck space than inside living space. Located on Horsehead Bay in Puget Sound it provides swimmers and sailors with a dressing room and bathroom, and a small kitchenette for preparation of informal meals.

A large deck surrounds the glass-walled front of the cabin, and wide doors open from the main room onto the deck. In the center of the living room a buoy-shaped metal fireplace radiates heat on all sides.

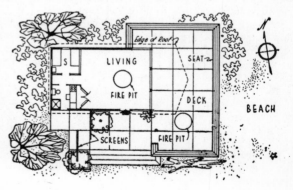

FIREWOOD *is stored in open area under the cabin. Note enclosed storeroom at the far right, lower corner.*

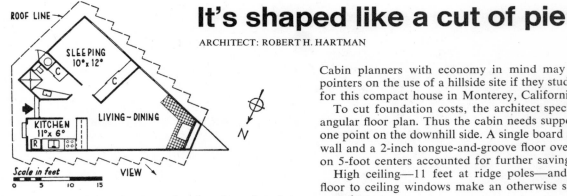

PLAN *lets bathroom, fireplace absorb awkward angles.*

It's shaped like a cut of pie

ARCHITECT: ROBERT H. HARTMAN

Cabin planners with economy in mind may get some pointers on the use of a hillside site if they study the plan for this compact house in Monterey, California.

To cut foundation costs, the architect specified a triangular floor plan. Thus the cabin needs support at only one point on the downhill side. A single board and batten wall and a 2-inch tongue-and-groove floor over joists set on 5-foot centers accounted for further savings.

High ceiling—11 feet at ridge poles—and plenty of floor to ceiling windows make an otherwise small room seem larger.

LOOKING *from fireplace toward kitchen pass-through.*

FIREPLACE *has raised tile hearth that's also a seat.*

SUN DECK *built at back of cabin, above car port, has canvas laced on a pipe frame for sun and wind control.*

Summer comfort on a mountain lake

ARCHITECT: JOE B. WOOD

SLIDING GLASS WALL *opens living room to terrace.*

SNACK BAR *separates the kitchen from the living room.*

On Lake Chelan in eastern Washington, this summer cabin works so well the owners and their family wouldn't mind having an all-year house just like it.

Some of the features of the plan which make waterfront living simple and easy are: 1) A masonry core with two fireplaces, one opening into the living room and the other onto the terrace. 2) An extra entry through the bathroom so that sand-covered sun bathers can take a foot bath or shower before entering the main cabin. 3) Good traffic planning — several entries, not just one. In the kitchen the appliances are lined up against one wall so through traffic to bedrooms will not interfere with the cook. 4) Durable, rough materials which require little maintenance.

The cabin sits on a shelf bulldozed from a sloping site. The designer has given it the snugness and the trim lines of a ship — from the flagpole in front to the sun deck that stretches out over the carport.

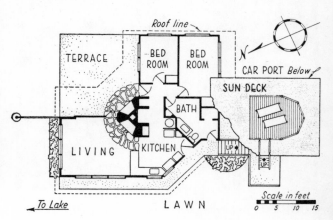

TRIANGULAR DECK *follows the contour of the land. It is off main room, on sunny, private side of cabin.*

Compact cabin on an island

ARCHITECT: ALAN RAE

Like a bird's nest, this small cabin perches above heavy growth of ferns, goldenrod, tiger lilies and other Northwest native plants on Washington's Whidbey Island. But all the cabin essentials have been packed inside the 18 by 20-foot space.

Several factors helped to keep the costs down. A simple box plan (relieved only by the roof line) was used. Inexpensive materials were chosen to carry out the plan.

The owners worked weekends, doing for themselves such labor as digging ditches for plumbing, installing wiring, and taking care of most of the finishing details.

The front windows are fixed so ventilation comes through the open door. Clerestory window (note top of picture at right) runs the entire width of the house, lets in the east morning sun and provides a balance to the interior lights during the remainder of the day.

COOKING CORNER *is compact and efficient in design.*

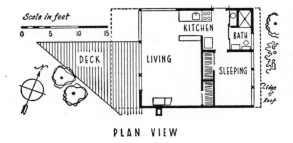

PLAN VIEW

CUSTOM CABINS
Saltwater Shores

North from Point Conception to the Canadian border, the rugged Pacific shore is dotted with cabins. Mists may roll shoreward all summer long and howling storms batter the bluffs in winter, but the long strip is a favored retreat for cabin dwellers who like to be within earshot of the pounding surf.

The allure is the same one oceans have always had. There are fish to be caught, beaches to be combed, tidepools to be watched, and unknown horizons to be thought about.

The cabins tend to be low-lying buildings, left unpainted to weather, and designed specifically to be snug and warm on nights when all deckhands to west are muttering and cursing the fates that put them out to sea in such weather.

FIVE-FOOT-WIDE *deck surrounds cabin, nearly flush with adjoining concrete slab that helps extend outdoor living area. Cabin rotates so slowly that even small children can ride on and off the deck.*

It turns like a giant lazy Susan

ARCHITECT: HAROLD BARTRAM

Flip a switch and this cabin on Blakely Island, Washington, turns like a giant lazy Susan to catch the sun or view. It rides on eight plastic-faced wheels that run on a steel track bolted to a circular track. Two of the wheels are powered by a ¾-horse reversible gear motor controlled through low-voltage switching.

THE OWNERS *fly here in 1½ hours from Kent, Oregon.*

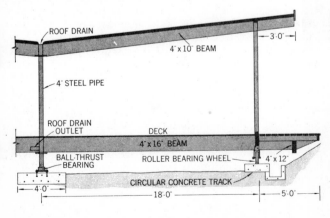

CABIN *turns 270° on central steel column on ball-thrust bearing. Flexible sections in water, sewer lines.*

CABIN *is then rotated so living room faces the sun.*

DECK IS A JUMP *and a dive from lakeshore, and not much more distant from ocean surf. Decks are efficient means of keeping sand out of interior—especially if boards are spaced. View is from bedroom wing.*

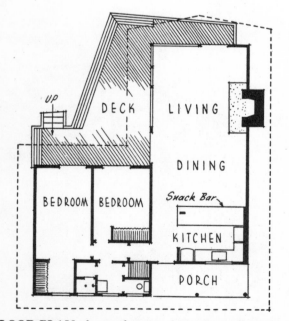

FLOOR PLAN *shows absence of interior walls, a boon when rain keeps owners indoors all weekend. Doors lead directly to bedrooms for returning swimmers.*

This cabin is built

ARCHITECT: GEORGE T. ROCKRISE

Along much of the Pacific shore, it may rain steadily for a week, and be overcast and foggy for even longer. That sort of weather has its own allure, and then there is the sudden appearance of blue skies, with warm sun tempered by gentle breezes. It is a joyous change.

The Oregon coast south of Bandon experiences these whimsies, and the architect planned this cabin to make the best of all sides of a moody climate.

For balmy days, there is a sizeable deck. It is only a few steps away from a small lake (Floras), and a hundred yards away from the surf on the far side of a sandspit.

For indoor days, the cabin has generous open space within its walls. The absence of partitions in the living-dining-kitchen area, and in the dormitory, keeps the cabin from seeming cramped even if the rains do not go away to await another day. A bonus was a substantial reduction in per-square-foot building costs.

The exterior is cedar siding. The roof is of shakes. Stone for the massive fireplace was gathered on site.

GLASS-WALLED LIVING ROOM *is comfortable vantage for viewing swirling storms as they rush ashore. The couches are fine for lazy day lounging, can double as extra sleeping space when guests are on hand.*

where weather is whimsical

BREAKFAST COUNTER *and rustic picnic table are handy to kitchen, plentiful seating for a full house. All furnishings are rustic, easy to keep clean.*

MASSIVE FIREPLACE *has heat vents in sides, a major source of warmth in the cabin. Intakes are near floor level; outlet vents are just above damper level.*

FROM BALCONY, *fireplace is focal point. Steps down to recess serve as seating. Kerosene lamp is light.*

An away-from-it-all vacation house

ARCHITECTS: WILKINS-ELLISON

FLOOR PLAN *is of first floor. Balcony, above kitchen, is divided into two equal sleeping rooms.*

The idea is to get away from it all, and the owners of this cabin on the shores of Puget Sound in Washington succeed at just that.

There is a well, but no running water. There is no electricity, no telephone.

The building, just out of reach of storm waves, is a design of such universal flavor that it has been likened to Samoan thatched huts, Mayan residences, and indigenous Indian architecture.

Key element seems to be the tall roof, which gives room for a sleeping balcony and a lofty main living room, as well as lending architectural distinction.

Inside, the scissors trusses that support the roof are indeed Samoan.

The fireplace is as much talked-about as the style of the building. It has the same sort of charm as the outdoor campfire circle, and its sizeable hood provides radiated heating all the way to its top.

Wood window panels close the cabin tight.

DINING AREA *is separated from living room by its elevation, even with the outside deck level.*

SAND PILED *high in three-legged brazier insulates floor from heat of fire. Fireplace is sole heat source.*

KITCHEN IS COMPACT, *centers around wood stove. Above, bedrooms open onto living room, fireplace.*

WOOD PANELS *tuck under eaves when cabin is in use, are easily lowered to close vacant cabin tight.*

SKYLIGHTS *in roof are visible in this view of cabin after owners have closed it before leaving.*

FROM ROAD, *outline of the building echoes the slanting line of the cliff beyond, secludes owners from view.*

Open but private...small but spacious

ARCHITECT: JAMES CHARLTON

TERRACE, *a sunny-climate walled patio, cuts force of sea breezes. Tapered walls are self-bracing.*

The lesson of this beach house is that simple materials and forms can produce an exciting structure, and that a small space can be livable.

The frame is simple post and beam. The walls are glass and stucco. The main floor is brick laid dry over a slab. The bedrooms are a balcony above the carport. The patio is brick laid in sand, and sheltered by extensions of the stucco walls.

It is tucked on a narrow beach below cliffs at Malibu, California.

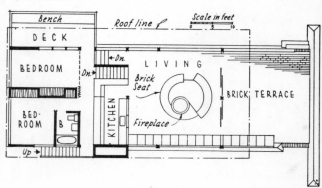

SPACIOUSNESS *in a small building is achieved by raising level of bedrooms to a balcony.*

DRAMATIC LIVING ROOM *focuses on fireplace with built-in seats around it. Terrace doubles apparent size.*

BEDROOM BALCONY *offers a wholly private vantage for enjoyment of view. Overhang shades it.*

KITCHEN *is part of main living room, but storage and serving counter screens any clutter.*

SIX-FOOT SIDE WALLS *are blank, with high windows above, assurance of privacy from adjoining cabins. Bedroom wing is the foreground structure. Ocean is beyond; Bolinas Lagoon is to rear in this view of cabin.*

Here are ideas to study...

ARCHITECT: SHERWOOD STOCKWELL

On the ocean side of the spit that separates Bolinas Lagoon from the Pacific near Stinson Beach, California, this small cabin makes the most of its location.

It delivers the fun the idea of a beach house promises. Its four-gable roof has a jaunty air as it opens the house to the scenery of rolling hills. Its windows look right out on the beach, or into a sandy play-yard court. Its doors open onto decks a step up from beach or court. The house is warm and sheltering when ocean fogs or storms roll in, a seat before its fireplace a fine refuge from any damp chilliness in the air.

The house solves or minimizes the problems of beach living. Sitting on a platform above ground, it is easy to care for as little sand tracks indoors. Its wings shelter it from winds and curious onlookers without inhibiting the views of sea, hills, or sky. Facing south, it suffers little afternoon glare. High gable windows balance bright light from sea and sand.

FROM ENTRY DECK, *view is through living room to sea beyond. Wide-spaced deck boards help get sand off feet before it gets tracked inside. Bedrooms at right.*

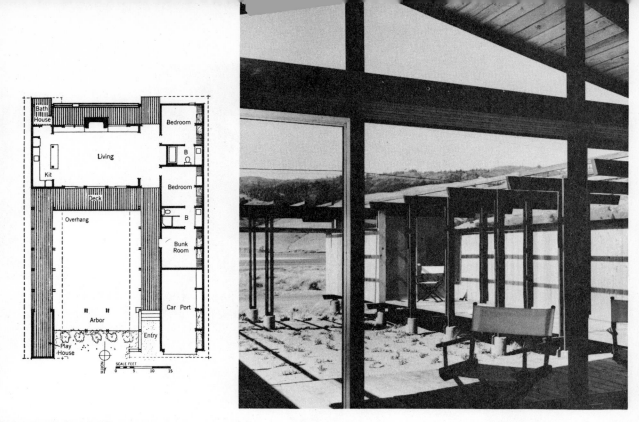

BUILDING IS U-SHAPED, *living area is L-shaped as plan shows. Picture (right) shows side wall that makes "U." Topped by pergola, it has playhouse at end for rainy days. View is toward the lagoon from living room.*

if you dream of a house by the beach

COMPACT KITCHEN *is open to living room, but partly screened by cabinets and serving counter. Bath house is through door at right side of kitchen.*

LIGHTS AT NIGHT *reveal the floating effect of the four-gable roof. Fireplace is in ocean-facing window wall. Its raised hearth extends as bench.*

TILTED CABIN *focuses on ocean view like a camera, has room for car and boat storage beneath high side.*

Beach house aimed at the view

ARCHITECTS: LIDDLE & JONES

DRAWING MATCHES *perspective of photo, shows how all levels benefit from sea view.*

It looks a bit like a missile on its launching pad, but the cabin's purpose is really the reverse: To keep the owners in close touch with their earthly and attractive surroundings on Washington's Puget Sound.

The uncommon design serves to solve two fairly common waterside problems: Close neighbors, and glare off water and sand.

The architects avoided side windows that might look out on an adjoining house, not built when the photos were made but soon to come.

Tilting the house avoided sun glare, with the aid of long, low eaves that function as eyebrows. This device helps exploit the water view in the absence of side windows. The interior has three open levels, each with a view of beach and water. The levels separate living spaces without need for inside walls.

Sheathing beneath the shingles is diagonal, structurally designed to permit the 12-foot cantilever of the sleeping area over the carport. The cantilever reaches out from a concrete block basement that houses utilities, furnace.

LIVING ROOM, *at deck level, has built-in seating on both side walls, sliding doors on end wall.*

SOUTH-FACING DECK *is a sun-trap in winter. Living room windows behind are only side-facing ones.*

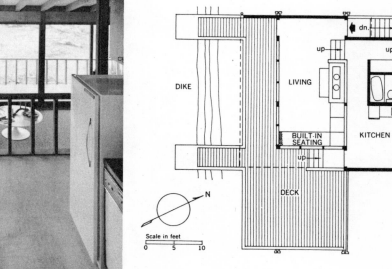

VIEW THROUGH KITCHEN *from sleeping level. Bedrooms can be made private by drawing draperies.*

ENCLOSED SPACE *is only 900 square feet. Sleeping rooms are at high end. Living room level with deck.*

SLEEPING ALCOVES—*one shows at right—double as lounging areas during the day. Easy access to deck enhances sense of spaciousness in the small room. Floor lamps mounted on corner posts illuminate ceiling.*

A 1-room, 5-room beach house

ARCHITECTS: OSBORNE & STEWART

ROOMY DECK *adds 650 square feet to useful space of cabin. Two sets of stairs lead to ground level.*

If this whimsical little cabin looks like driftwood tossed up on the beach after a winter storm, then its architects succeeded.

The owner asked for a weather-beaten treasure that would live up to a name like "The Lookout."

It is a simple structure, designed to be built by semi-skilled hands. For this reason its cost was a surprisingly low $5,000, including architects' fees. The figure could have been doubled with more refined detailing requiring master craftsmen.

Its designers described it as a "one-room, five-room cabin" using a cruciform plan with poles at the indented corners. Essentially it is one room separated into two sleeping alcoves, a kitchen-bath alcove, and a central sitting area, all in a space of fewer than 450 square feet.

The cabin is up on poles because the lot, once fronting on the water of Bodega Bay, is cut off from the shore by a new road that has to be overlooked. The architects figured that this approach added about $300 to the overall cost.

Other economies compensated for that expense. All of the doors and windows and some of the plumbing materials were bought from a wrecking company for less than $150. Hardware is all of the most economical sort.

KITCHEN ALCOVE *takes up hardly more space than a closet, is well-lighted day or night.*

JAUNTY FEELING *of cabin is apparent from outside. Carport, storage units use ground space fully.*

built for only $5,000

And the hearth beneath the metal fireplace is a wood frame filled with dry-laid brick.

The roof, ordinary enough in appearance from without, is an unusual one. It is formed by 32 radial rafters bolted to a metal compression ring in the center. The perimeter beams are 4 by 12's, which are bolted to the upright poles at each corner.

The walls are redwood. Floor and decking are of edge-laid Douglas fir 2 by 4's. The poles are pressure-treated commercial pilings.

The jaunty crown atop the flue is a 50-gallon oil drum, originally acquired as a caisson to support sand while posts were being set.

ON GROUND HIGH ENOUGH TO SEE WATER BEYOND ROAD

DECK HIDES ROAD *from view, brings the cabin into contact with Bodega Bay beach beyond.*

ECONOMICAL CABINS
Owner-builts, Stock Plans

Most of us cannot afford the delicious luxury of planning and building a cabin precisely to suit every need, and exercise man's old urge to construct his own shelter.

But it wouldn't be the West if there weren't a sizable number of such hardy and independent spirits around, dotting the landscape with the direct and honest sort of buildings that give the region much of its flavor.

It is no easy matter to solve all the problems inherent in doing something in a place chosen because it is away from convenience. The record assembled in the following pages shows that, not only can a man succeed, he can achieve considerable style.

THIS CABIN *perches in the hau trees overlooking Kaneohe Bay. Prevailing wind hits far side of the roof.*

VIEW WALL *of living and sleeping area covered only with screening; two panels open in the center.*

Cabin in the hau trees

You can tell this cabin is in Hawaii. One whole wall is nothing but screening. In bad weather it rains in sometimes, but the owners have the option of putting windows in.

This is a cabin to induce a mood of relaxation. It also shows what can be done in a very small space and with little furniture. It includes the requisites of a pleasant weekend in a main floor just 20 by 22 feet. The architect-owner, Richard N. Dennis, and his wife built it themselves, with five days' worth of hired help on the footing and framings.

The cabin is a platform anchored to the hillside along the wall where you enter. It perches on a steep bank, with a stairway built down to the shore. That the stairway is reached by a trap door in the upper floor only adds to the romance. A lower level takes advantage of the space below with a screened enclosure for an extra bed.

This cabin has screened openings between the five-foot side walls and the roof to catch prevailing winds. On the mainland, ventilation may be less important, but it would still be fortunate to find a site with a breeze from one side, not from the direction of the sea view.

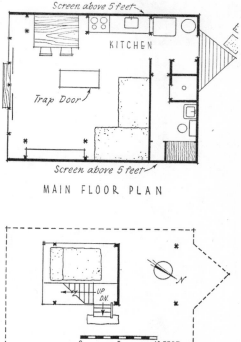

Screen above 5 feet

KITCHEN

Trap Door

Screen above 5 feet

MAIN FLOOR PLAN

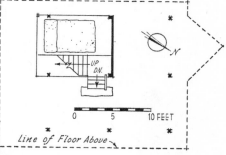

UP
DN.

N

0   5   10 FEET

Line of Floor Above

LOWER FLOOR PLAN

TEPEE CABIN *perches about 8 feet off ground. If enclosed, space below could be all-year work or storage area.*

VERTICAL DOOR *and window panel fits one of eight sides, provides shelter for storing skis, poles, firewood.*

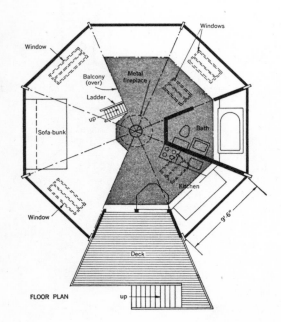

Tepee cabin

Snug in the snows of Snoqualmie Pass in the Washington Cascades, this octagonal pyramid ski cabin takes the principle of the A-frame a step further: It has no roof—or no walls, if you will—for about as economical a form as can be built. The 480-square foot main floor contains a living-sleeping area, kitchen, bath, plus another 100 square feet of sleeping balcony—enough for four sleeping bags. A third story contains a 97-square foot storage attic. Cabin sleeps 8-12 people for a ski weekend.

The cabin consists of the frame and insulated stressed-skin panels for floor, wall, door, and window units, all of which bolt together. Cabin cost: About $4,000, including foundation, fireplace, plumbing, kitchen, and electricity. Shell alone costs about half this total.

Design is by Virginia Lee.

METAL FIREPLACE *in center serves as heat source supplemented by electric heaters. Kitchen area at rear.*

HINGED *to wall and supported by chains, back of sofa becomes upper bunk; books (see below) now on edge.*

for ski weekends

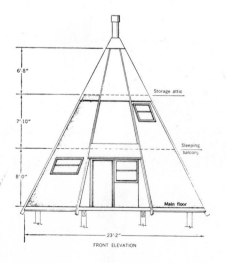

FRONT ELEVATION

6'-8"

7'-10"

8'-0"

Storage attic

Sleeping balcony

Main floor

23'-2"

DURING *the day the bunks fold down to make a sofa. Air mattresses are used for the seat and the back.*

ONE-ROOM INTERIOR *is divided with folding screens and two 6-foot partitions. One of the partitions is used as a wardrobe, one is a kitchen cupboard. Beds are on left wall and far end. Kitchen is located on left.*

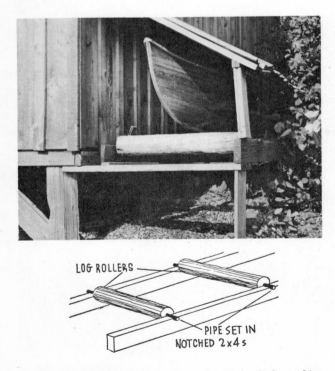

BOAT SHELTER *is located at the end of the cabin. The rollers make it easy to move the boat in and out.*

One big open room

Located only a short way downhill from their home, this cabin provides the owners and their family some priceless summer fun.

The cabin is 20-by-30 feet, built of ¾-inch cedar boards and battens with a shingle roof. It is set on a post and pier foundation. The sliding front walls are on roller skate wheels on a track at floor level outside the cabin.

Materials cost less than $1,000.

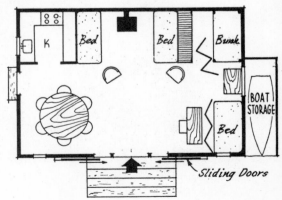

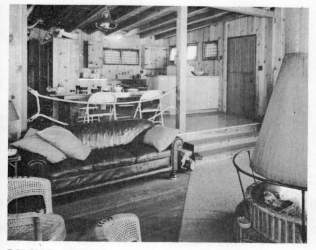

LIVING AREA *is on a lower level to fit slope of site. Main entry is Dutch door near the kitchen-dining area.*

FROM THE LAKE *side showing the deck. The latticed extension of the roof overhang helps shade the windows.*

VIEW FROM *dining area is of deck and lake. Windows have bamboo screens above center, draperies below.*

Split level on a slope

Designing and building this cabin on the Oregon coast was a labor of love and the cabin shows it. After the plans had been carefully worked out, the owners and one carpenter spent two weeks and a few extra weekends putting up the basic structure. Once this was done, the owner and his family began to put on all the finishing touches in their spare time.

The cabin is only 45 minutes from their home, and they use it on weekends as often as they can.

GALVANIZED HOOD *of expanded shale block fireplace drops down to start fire and to contain coals at night.*

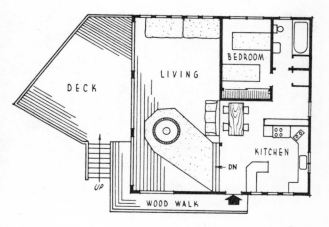

10:45 A.M., SATURDAY. *The owners started with the cabin's simple wood foundations. A tent (not shown) was used as a "construction camp."*

3:30 P.M., SATURDAY. *Walls, ceiling are in place. Combination folding wall and deck hinged to bottom of frame which sits level on concrete blocks.*

5:00 P.M., SUNDAY. *The kitcher pantry is equipped and ready to us Corrugated plastic overhead is attache to top of frame with piano hinge*

An expandable "core"

After many years of more conventional camping, the owners of the structure pictured here decided they needed a permanent camp where they could "settle down" for weekends and vacations. The sketch at the left shows how the cabin would look when completed. The owners prefabricated it in their basement during the winter. With the help of their two sons, they took it to the site . . . next to a mountain river, about 80 miles from their home. Cost of the entire project: about $350.

PLASTIC PANEL *is folded down while the roof work is finished. Roof framing was all pre-cut and ready to put in place to speed up this task.*

THE CABIN *in action: Roof over the "front porch" is supported by two aluminum poles. Bedroom addition is identical but on other side of the frame.*

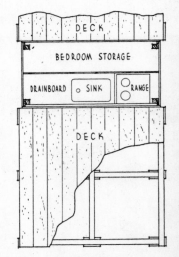

CABIN FLOOR PLAN. *The found tion for the hinged floor is made of 6 6 cedar timbers. Saplings were lean against frame for snow protectic*

THE KITCHEN *is very simple at first with dishwashing facilities and a window on right wall to be added.*

HERE PANELS *are open at each end. This is the "living" end, the kitchen is on the other side of fireplace.*

BEDS ARE *located on either side of the fireplace. There is also an upper bunk above bed on the far side.*

SHOWN ABOVE *is cabin with the end panels closed. Panels have a hollow core and are faced with hardboard.*

Pivoting walls, big deck

The way this cabin works best is shown in the plan on the right. Basically it is a box with end walls made of pivoting panels which open to three generous decks.

The deck and cabin floor are of 2 by 4's on edge. The roof is sheets of corrugated steel.

Of special interest is the raised T-shaped platform which has a fireplace in the center and beds on each side. A canvas behind the fireplace drops down to separate the two areas.

The cabin is located on the edge of a lake. Access is by boat. Cost of materials: about $1,200, all of which were floated in when construction took place.

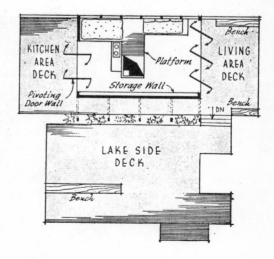

This A-frame cabin

Simplicity and strength combine with ample space and a sweeping view in this two-story A-frame shelter on Puget Sound.

The interior (700 square feet) is roomy enough for weekend entertaining. Decks on both levels nearly double the usable floor space, and generous use of glass both upstairs and down permits an overall effect of spaciousness. Kitchen, bath, living room, and a small corner for bed space are on the first floor; there are two dormitory-type bedrooms upstairs, plus a closet nearly 8 feet wide.

Dr. David Hellyer, who designed the cabin, had economy in mind as well as ease of construction when he limited the foundation to just nine concrete piers. The cabin's shape is formed by two frames consisting of heavy end beams joined at the top by conventional notching and slipping together of 4 by 6's, followed by spiking. Much of the construction work can be done by owners with some basic building knowledge and aptitude, but professional help is advisable in the early stages as well as with wiring and the installation of plumbing and fixtures.

Although designed primarily for vacations and weekends, there is easily enough floor space to qualify this cabin for year-around use. Also, because of its design and its rigid construction, this cabin withstands snow and would make a good mountain shelter.

This building is fairly typical of one for which stock plans are available. A list of sources of stock plans is to be found on page 110.

FRONT VIEW *of cabin. Stairway at right of windows has hand rail for safety, leads from lower to upper deck.*

DECK EXTENDS *nearly 9 feet past cabin door. Lumber for the 16-foot-wide deck is 2 by 6's, spaced ½ inch.*

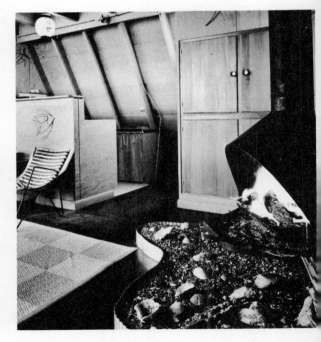

HUB OF ACTIVITY *on rainy days is metal fireplace. Aluminum garden edging contains gravel "beach."*

is a double decker

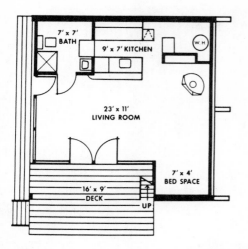

FIRST FLOOR plan. Note single-door side entry from the narrow deck along left side of cabin.

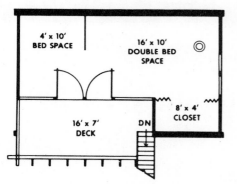

SECOND FLOOR plan. Deck has ¾-inch plywood panels; a weatherproofing agent was applied.

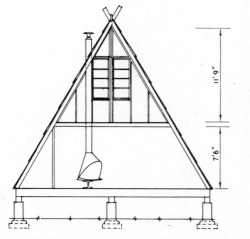

"WALK-AROUND" space is mostly in the downstairs area, because of the cabin roof's 60° pitch.

REAR VIEW shows roof of ⅜-inch exterior type fir plywood panels lapped like giant shingles.

LEFT: Foundation has nine concrete piers in rows of three, 12 feet apart. Each row supports an 8 by 10-inch beam 28-feet long. Professional help is advised.

RIGHT: Sub-flooring for first floor is of ¾-inch fir plywood over 2-by-12 floor joists and 2-by-4 blocking. Second floor joists are all 3 by 8's.

CABIN'S PEAKED ROOF *has the look of a hat at a rakish angle. A two-way fireplace could be added on this side (see plan); this would enhance the interior and also provide a handsome outdoor brick barbecue.*

Low cost leisure...with lots of room

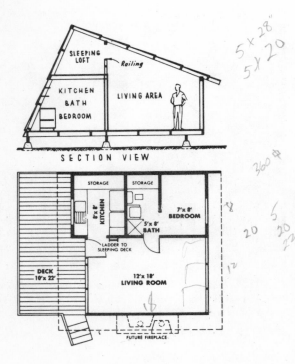

This cabin interior was designed for 400 square feet, counting the open half-attic. Outside, the deck adds another 220 square feet across the entire front of the cabin. The 12 by 18-foot living room is bigger than those in many of today's tract homes. The bedroom is ample by cabin standards, and it adjoins the bathroom (via a folding door) to make a suite. The kitchen has walking and turn-around space and plenty of room for opening refrigerator and oven doors. The attic loft serves as an extra sleeping area; some or all of this deck can be put to good use for storage. Two other important space factors: the roof's pitch means there's plenty of overhead room within and there are many possibilities for future expansion.

The structure rests on a concrete block foundation. Floor joists supporting the plywood floor panels are 2 by 8's; the decking and the wall studs are 2 by 4's; roof joists are 2 by 6's. Wall siding and roof are ⅜-inch fir plywood panels. The roof panels are lapped like shingles. Siding is nailed directly to the studs. Joints of the plywood panels which form the roof and siding are covered with battens, sealed with non-hardening mastic for protection against water.

This cabin was designed by Architect Walter D. Widmeyer. Part of the basic concept is easy construction, so site owners can buy a stock plan and work from there. For a list of stock plan sources, see page 110.

SUB-FLOORING *is ¾-inch fir ply nailed to floor joists. It could also rest on pre-cast concrete piers.*

ROOF PITCH *is steep. The roof joists are covered with an exterior type fir plywood sheathing.*

PANELS *are lapped over lower sections. The simple design allows for some off-site fabrication.*

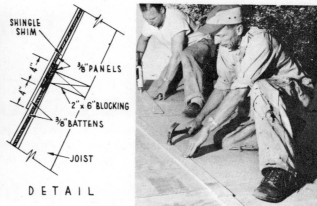

PLYWOOD BATTENS *are nailed over joints between panels. Note how panel overlaps, shown in detail drawing.*

BATHROOM *has stall shower, no tub. Paneling is a hard surface, high density overlaid fir plywood.*

LARGE WINDOWS *brighten cabin's interior. Air from ventilating louvers is controlled by half-doors.*

INTERIOR *at the final stage, with cabin complete. Balcony which serves as entrance hall to the bedrooms also diminishes the height of inside wall to the scale of the fireplace and hearth. Room size is 15 by 27 feet.*

A cabin to be built in 4 stages

Planning a cabin, a summer vacation shack, a place in the country, used to be a normal and familiar activity. Families who still want to tackle a cabin themselves should first consider the differences between a cabin and a house:
1. More than a house, the cabin lends itself to piecemeal building—a stage-by-stage development with livability at every stage.
2. Skilled workmanship is not necessary in the cabin. Rough construction is in tune with cabin living.
3. Many steps in cabin building are in the capacity range of the amateur builder.

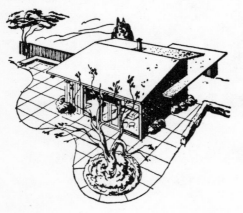

4. If the use of the cabin is concentrated in the summer months, costs of providing space for sleeping and entertaining can be held to the minimum.

A hypothetical family (two teen-age boys) has bought three acres of woodland. They hope to build a cabin-lodge. A cost estimate on their rough plans has just come in and they find that financing is not to be had. What to do? Shall they build a permanent camp this summer? Or try to build a cabin on a pay-as-you-go basis?

Here are the answers Architect George T. Rockrise of San Francisco gave them:
1. Set up a five-year building program aimed at a cabin which will be drawn up in complete detail now.
2. Each of four stages of development will be complete in itself. If at the end of the second year you wish to postpone the next step for a year or more, you will have a usable and livable summer unit.
3. Each yearly addition will be made without remodeling or re-doing any previous work.
4. The cabin design will avoid special building skills. Methods will be standard and universally understood.
5. All materials—windows, doors, glass, kitchen-bathroom equipment—are generally available in economical stock sizes.
6. Expenditure will be budgeted in equal yearly payments.

FIRST STAGE

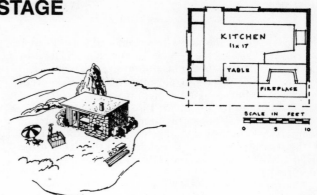

The kitchen comes first for many reasons—economies in food, time saved in preparing meals for hungry and busy builders. The kitchen is large enough for a storm refuge or for family gatherings. It serves as a storage area. Kitchen plus fireplace plus canvas adds up to a lot of convenience.

Those who favor the half camp, half cabin idea could stop building here, or after any later stage.

In the first year the cabin is little more than a camp with a deluxe family-size kitchen. However, a smart use of canvas roofing extending from the kitchen with canvas walls at one or two sides would give adequate living space in summer months or convert large areas into usable space for sleeping quarters.

SECOND STAGE

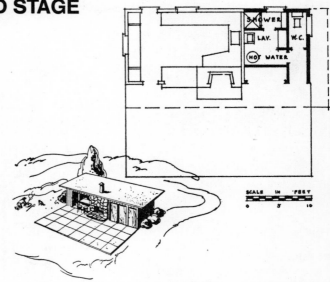

With the addition of a water system and a bathroom the camp becomes civilized. So here the problems of water supply and storage, water heating, septic tank and electrical power system must be solved, and are a large part of the construction at this stage of development.

Hot water coils in the fireplace provide one source of hot water. If a better than average supply of sunlight is available, solar heating is another possible source.

The bath is compartmented to handle three people at a time. With a bathroom added to the kitchen, the utility core of the cabin is complete.

It is wise in the second stage to complete a concrete slab foundation that will allow a smooth dry area in front of the fireplace and add livability to that area.

The concrete slab is a base for additional shelters. If the site is fairly level and transportation not too expensive, a concrete slab simplifies construction. A rented concrete mixer and the division of slab into sections by headers will overcome obvious objections in working with large areas of concrete.

THIRD STAGE

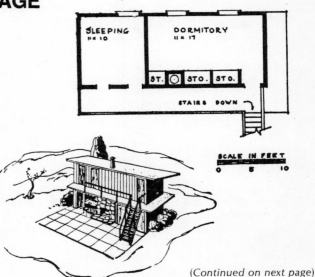

The progress plan of the building was designed to allow either the living room or the bedrooms to come first. Which should be built now is purely a family preference. If bedrooms are the choice see plan at left. Note that two doors lead into the sleeping room shown in the plan. The one farthest left is for access from bedroom to a future closet. This will be built on the end of balcony when the fourth stage of construction (the living room) commences.

If the choice is to build the living room in the third stage, the wall between living and sleeping rooms will be the outside wall until those rooms are built. The chimney flue will be left exposed.

A patented fireplace form with circulating warm air has been specified here for the reason that it takes the difficulties out of fireplace building. Amateur builders are not likely to make a mistake in the design of the working parts of the fireplace with such a unit.

(Continued on next page)

FOURTH STAGE

The overhang of the first kitchen unit now serves as a balcony hallway to the bedrooms. Amount and size of glass would depend on the maximum size the builder can handle. Crystal sheet will be satisfactory in the 6-foot 6-inch spaces indicated in the plan. However, wood members can be adjusted to provide for smaller glass units.

After the completion of the fourth stage, all the interior living space is finished. This much cabin can provide most of the comforts of home. Depending on the site and the owner's desires will determine whether or not outdoor additions will be made.

A note about siding and roofing: Rough 1-inch boards will serve well if used with battens or weatherproofing. Nail building paper on the studs. There are many grades of building paper, some with a metal finish on one side, which are not unattractive left exposed. If more insulation is desirable, finish later with boards, plywood, or composition panels.

An optional fifth stage calls for additions of carport and storage at back right corner of cabin.

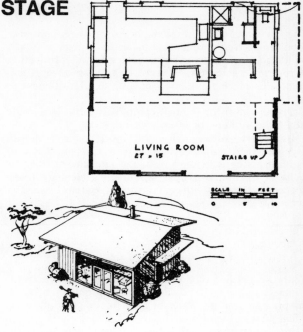

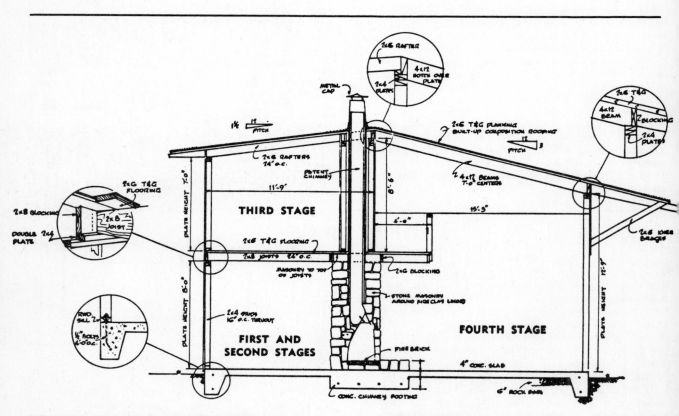

HOW THE FRAME IS PUT TOGETHER: With few exceptions, the first three stages could be handled by one man working alone. (A power saw would be highly desirable.) But in the fourth stage, extra hands will be needed for 4 by 12-inch beams.

In the first and second stages, 2 by 6-inch tongue-and-groove planking serves as the roof. Rolled roofing laid on top will be adequate for two or three years. Then when you add the bedrooms, just take up the roofing and this planking is your floor. Tongue-and-groove gives such strong bracing there is no need to apply in on the diagonal as with shiplap.

Cabin on stilts-$2,500

View property "too steep to build on" is common in many prime vacation areas. But here is a cabin that can go on practically anything short of a cliff. It was built on a 45° slope overlooking Hood Canal in Washington. The nearest road access was 200 feet up the hill.

A structural engineer designed the cabin himself. In his basement in Tacoma, using materials costing less than $2,500 total, he prefabricated all the components so that nothing would involve more than a two-man carry. Plywood floor sections fastened to 2 by 4 joists came in 4-foot-square units; hollow-box beams of plywood weighed less than 100 pounds. The walls and the folded plate roof were also plywood. (The folded plate roof bears its own weight and holds the walls together.)

Then the owner hauled everything in one truckload to the drop-off point on the access road, where six friends helped him slide it down to the site and erect the entire cabin in six weekends.

None of the prefabricated elements of floor, wall, roof, or support is radically new in principle or design. Many building contractors are familiar with all of them. You can get an architect or structural engineer—or both to help you design or modify it to fit a particular site.

36-FOOT DECK *runs along front of cabin. Underneath, hollow-box beams rest on stiltlike underpinning; at rear they rest on hillside. Note stairs at left.*

LIVING ROOM *before it was painted. There are also a kitchen, two bedrooms, and bath. This end of the deck (behind sliding doors) is 8 feet wide and 18 feet long.*

WALL SECTION *components were nailed together on cabin floor, tilted up and propped in place for nailing. There was no electricity so power tools weren't used.*

ECONOMICAL CABINS
Pre-fabs and Pre-cuts

The preceeding section notes that independent spirits going their own way have contributed much to cabin architecture and their own pleasure in the West.

A substantial industry has grown out of that sort of spirit. It is the pre-fab and pre-cut cabin industry, which permits independence even among those who have not the draughting skills to do their own design.

None of the pains and pleasures of the physical labor are gone, but a great deal of arithmetic is. Most pre-fabs have complete wall sections, while pre-cuts are entirely loose lumber. A good many pre-fab shells can be erected in a weekend, although the plumbing and wiring will require professional help, and the finishing inside will remain to be done.

Built in 2 weeks

TRUCK UNLOADED *pieces a half mile from cabin site. It took 15 loads with a pickup to move it into place. All pieces were in shipment; all fit together well.*

On-site camping by the owners, plus the help of several friends got the results pictured here. All of this was accomplished during a two-week vacation period.

The pre-fab cabin cost $1,850 FOB Kennydale, Washington (in 1955). Trucking the materials to the owner's site near La Honda (30 miles south of San Francisco) cost $400.

The owners experienced no trouble putting the cabin together, despite their unfamiliarity with such projects. They found that it was the kind of cabin they could use the year around.

FOUNDATION *is ready-made concrete piers set on concrete poured in holes dug down to a solid base. Note how corner pieces overlap. Dog was good tool carrier.*

FINAL STAGE—*as roof sheathing goes on. Pipes are on outside of single wall construction. Permanent camp was used while the cabin was being built.*

FINISHED CABIN—*later a fireplace was added to end wall at right. Owners cut trees to make the clearing. Weed killer was used to keep stumps flush with ground.*

IMMEDIATE OCCUPANCY *was a "must" for the owners of this cabin, who wanted to live in it while finishing it. Things to be done when they moved in were painting roof overhang, finishing porch paneling.*

A pre-fab case history

The owners of the cabin shown on these two pages believe the "pre-built" was their best buy, even though they had neither the time nor the inclination to do all the work themselves. For manpower they relied on the help of friends plus some paid professional help.

SETTING FOUNDATION *piers on pier footings was done after contractor laid out the exact position the week before. The owner dug the holes—saving $30. The contractor's price was only $20 more than if the owner had made them. Each pier weighs 25 pounds.*

As usual, there were unexpected problems:

The bulldozer, clearing for the access road, uncovered an abundant spring and the resulting stream of water had to be channeled around the house site. The truck delivering the cabin accidentally backed off the steep access road and half the cabin landed in the blackberry bushes (unharmed, fortunately). The portable gas generator which was brought along to run a power saw broke down.

Nevertheless, the problems were surmounted and the job got done. What's more, the owners still consider this their best possible bargain in a cabin.

Starting with the picture in the lower left hand corner on this page and continuing on the page opposite the sequence of 10 photographs shows the construction of the above pre-fab cabin over a span of five days.

The manufacturer agreed to supply help in the actual construction (at the standard wage rate) for as many days as might be needed. When the cabin was finished, including painting and cleaning up, the owners figured they and their friends had provided a little more than half of all the labor.

The cabin is 32 by 24 feet (including an 8 by 24-foot covered porch). The cabin shell, including interior partitions—but not interior finishing materials, plumbing, or wiring—cost approximately $2,500, delivered. The owner hired about $250 worth of expert help to put up the cabin shell.

He did the wiring himself because he had had experience in this field. The plumbing was installed by a contractor.

EACH PIER *footing is about 5 inches deep. Concrete is mixed and poured, then piers are laid on top when concrete is partially set up. The string in lower right corner outlines the walls of the house; outside piers must align.*

THE SITE *is uneven. To get right height for posts that support 4 by 6-inch floor joists, the builder extended leveled board from highest pier (on which no post will rest) measured the distance from it down to piers, and cut posts to fit.*

LOOKING DOWN *on building site with all but the last row of the floor joists in place. This is second day of construction; truck is backed up to site with a load of sub-floor boards. Drainage ditch carries water around site.*

TRIMMING *the 2 by 6-inch tongue and groove sub-floor (generator for power saw wasn't working yet) on morning of third day. The truck in the background is loaded up with half the cabin walls. The rest are up the hill.*

TWO MEN *can erect the 300-pound wall sections. Four make it easier. Walls wobble until corner sections are attached. Sections are nailed together down their length for snug fit. Plates overlap at the top and at the bottom.*

WALL SECTIONS *forming corner will stand alone while other walls are added, but the building isn't stable until gable ends and supporting beams are up. Whole aluminum sashes fit the pre-cut window openings.*

THREE *"slave laborers" and two "foremen" get a roof beam in place (there are two more men at the other end of the beam). This is one of two main roof beams running through the house, here being fitted into slot in end of gable.*

WITH ROOF *beams in place, rafters, supporting cross beams are added. Then roof is "sheeted" with plywood panels. Later, these were covered by composition shingles. Underside of plywood panels is textured and forms ceiling.*

THIS PHOTOGRAPH, *taken at same time as the one at left, shows sloping site, covered porch, interior partitions, method of roof construction. This was the fifth day. By dark roof panels were on, windows and doors in place.*

A potpourri of pre-fab ideas

What follows is a small introduction to the remarkable diversity in cabins offered to the public by pre-fab and pre-cut manufacturers and distributors.

Most of the cabins represented are from large firms, and as such are one among many models available. As the pre-fab business has grown, it has tended to concentrate increasingly in a few large firms that distribute all over the West, or at least in several states.

There are advantages. Mainly, large scale makes possible really efficient production of standard models. Also,

THE SIERRA   850 sq. ft.
ABC Package Homes, 2616 Springs Road, Vallejo, Calif. 94593. Forty models, from 375 square feet. Includes prefab walls; interior, exterior materials except rough plumbing, wiring, floors, painting, hot coat roof.

SEQUOIA   640 sq. ft.
Air-Lock Log Company, Box 1073, Prescott, Ariz. 86301. Fifty-nine models. Panels are available to design your own plan. Pre-cut logs for walls, gables, beams, rafters. Logs treated for protection against moisture, termites.

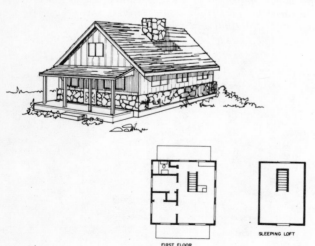

FIRST FLOOR

SLEEPING LOFT

THE SILVERLODE LODGE   1,238 sq. ft.
The Huntridge Corporation, Box 18574, Kearns Station, Salt Lake City, Utah 84118. Other models available, also custom designing and construction. Porch included in basic plan. Available extras: fireplace, kitchen and storage cabinets, interior finish materials.

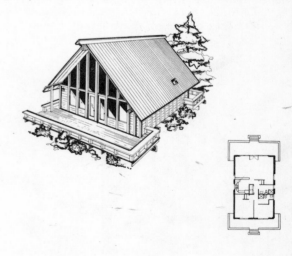

THE NOYO CHALET   1,422 sq. ft.
Union Lumber, Fort Bragg, Calif. 95437 (Write for complete information). Eight models from 846 square feet. Available in precut kit, prefab shell or completely constructed package. Lifetime interlocking redwood roof system, redwood exterior and interior walls.

these firms are geared to shipping their cabins over long distances, so the parts are packaged properly, and the rates are well known.

Many local firms augment the range of choice. These local operators offer some good buys, so long as the site is within their normal business area. Because they are small and local, many stay in the pre-fab business only for a few years, until the immediate market shrinks to an unprofitable level. In any event, canvass the local telephone books under the yellow page heading "Buildings—Pre-Cut and Pre-fabricated."

Any prospective pre-fab buyer will do well to shop around among all the competing firms to find the most suitable package, not only in terms of design and cost, but in such matters as assistance with labor, optional elements, and the like.

Most firms offer a range of choices beyond the mere shell. Some will include "package" plumbing or wiring. Some have options on windows, doors, interior walls, or interior modifications. It is wise to scout out the possibilities, keeping in mind your own skills, the skills of friends who can be drafted to help, the availability of local professional labor, the specific demands of your site on the design of the cabin, or the installation of utilities.

Each firm listed in this section will provide additional literature on request. (A small fee may be required.)

THE SEQUOIA

The Intermountain Company, Box 247, Auburn, Calif. 95603. Twenty-one models, particularly unusual A-frame

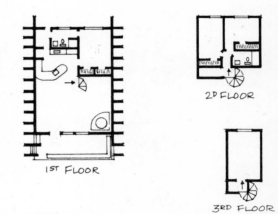

1,500 sq. ft.

adaptations. All models are insulated. Includes wrought iron spiral stairway, black metal fireplace. Spacious kitchen.

THE LEISURE   912 sq. ft.
Jim Walter Homes Corporation, Box 9128, Tampa, Fla. 33604. (Write for complete information on homes and financing.) Four models, custom constructed on your property. Features include hardboard siding, all aluminum windows and screens.

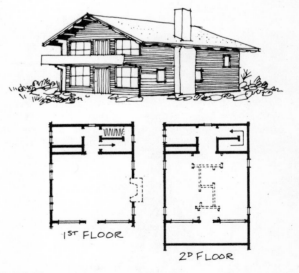

CHALET #500   1,000 sq. ft.
Justus Solid Cedar Homes, 2116 Taylor Way, Tacoma, Wash. 98421. Many models. Custom construction also. Double tongue and groove wall timbers and ceiling boards kiln dried. Dove-tail joints lock the corners and the partitions.

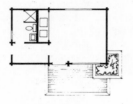

THE BACHELOR'S PAD   240 sq. ft.

K Products Corporation, 4940 Montecito, Santa Rosa, Calif. 95404. Many models. Includes everything from foundation up, except cabinets, plumbing, electrical and heating.

THE TAHOE   765 sq. ft

Lindal Cedar Homes, 9004 So. 19th St., Tacoma, Wash. Many models. Kiln dried Canadian Cedar. Includes everything from floor joists to roof. Not included paint, plumbing, electrical, heating, foundation materials

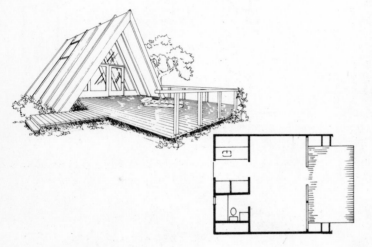

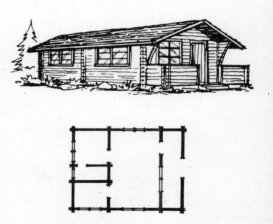

LEISURE HOUSE   432 sq. ft.

Campbell & Rocchia, 198 Francisco St., San Francisco, Calif. 94133. May be assembled by two people in a week, using only a hammer, saw, wrench and 12-foot ladder. Length may be added. Foundation not included.

MODEL #336   336 sq. ft.

Pan-Abode, 4350 Lake Washington Blvd., No. Renton Wash. 98055. One room cabins to large year-round homes Solid-wall construction. Cedar logs laid horizontally joined with tongue and groove.

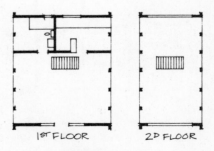

1ST FLOOR   2D FLOOR

HOLIDAY FRAME

Pierson Homes, 4100 Broadway, Eureka, Calif. 95501. Completely pre-cut, pre-drilled cabin shell. Redwood

688 sq. ft.

frame, foundation posts. Interior kit, plumbing kit, o electrical kit optional. Withstands heavy winds or snow

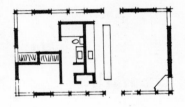

TIMBERLODGE

Pritchard Products Corporation, 4625 Roanoke Pkwy., Kansas City, Mo. 64112. Redwood log cabins,

720 sq. ft.

Chal-A. Basic module sections allow custom planning. Walls, doors, windows, roof sheathing, rafters supplied.

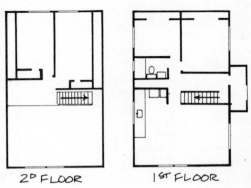

2ᴰ FLOOR   1ˢᵀ FLOOR

MATTERHORN

Manufactured Homes of California, 215 Exchange Ave., Fremont, Calif. 95448. Many other models. Includes pre-

1,436 sq. ft.

fab walls, interior, exterior materials. Not included: foundation, plumbing, wiring, heating, paint.

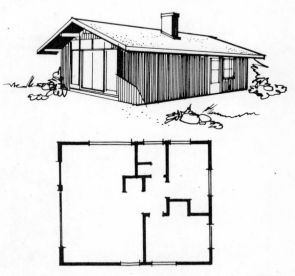

RETREAT   672 sq. ft.

Serendipity, 425 California Street, San Francisco, Calif. Other models. Choice of stage of completion: shell, semi-finished, or finished. Suitable for a vacation house or for permanent residency.

CHATHAM 28   672 sq. ft.

Techbuilt, 127 Mt. Auburn St., Cambridge, Mass. Many cabins, houses, custom designs. Includes panel wall sections, Douglas Fir posts and beams, rafters, plywood roof sheathing. Optional insulating, fireplace, appliances.

Inside Your Cabin

It used to be that most cabins were bare inside, to the point of being dreary. The notion was to minimize the housekeeping chores.

Happily, plastics, nylons, and other contributions of chemistry to convenience have given cabins a chance to be as handsome inside as out, without chaining the woman of the family to kitchen and broom.

Aside from minimizing nooks and crannies that are hard to clean, the main point of interior planning in a cabin is flexible accommodations. Most cabins tend to attract guests in greater numbers than the owner would ever have expected. So sleeping facilities ought to be expandable, and so should eating capacity. How comfortable the excess capacity is depends on the enthusiasm of the owner for his friends and family.

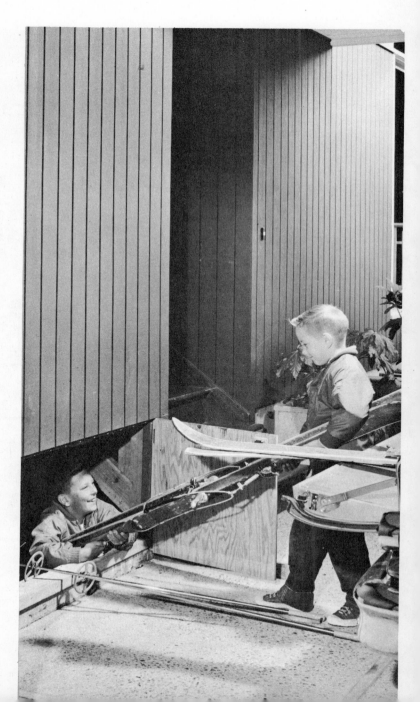

FOUR SETS *of bunks provide dormitory-type sleeping accommodations. Upper bunks, cantilevered from tops of built-in closets, are set back from bunks below by a third of their length. No need for support posts.*

Planning the cabin bedrooms

The vacation home must boast regular and emergency sleeping accommodations for a greater number than would be expected of a house in the city of the same size. This means careful planning to utilize all available space as economically and attractively as possible, without sacrificing comfort.

Double-purpose areas are usually the answer—beds in combination with sofas and storage units, or so designed that they may be brought out of hiding at a moment's notice.

Bunks may be built directly atop the other, or staggered to provide extra cupboard and drawer space as well as more head room at the lower level. Sofas that also serve as beds are particularly versatile, whether single or double. Good casters—hard-wheeled, ball-bearing types are best—make it easy to move large units.

Conceal one single bed under the other, to be rolled out when needed; or plan a corner arrangement of these two, perhaps with a square chest for blanket storage at their heads. A double bed may be pared down to sofa width by a back-rest storage unit; or the full size may be used as a wide lounge.

Porches, decks, and lofts make good sleeping spots, and Army bunks and cots are sturdy and inexpensive. Inner spring mattresses may be obtained in sizes to fit these cots, and the investment in extras is well worth while.

Metal bunks are cumbersome to move, but metal cots with folding legs and also those which fold in the middle are easily moved and stored. Canvas cots, though they are inclined to be cold and require extra padding for "insulation," can be knocked down into a bundle no larger than 37 by 8 by 4 inches. Sleeping bags and air mattresses are handy extras.

In considering location, remember it is easier to make a bed that can be approached from either side than one located in the corner of a room or in an alcove.

For early-morning comfort in the dressing area, provide a little electric heater or a portable kerosene stove

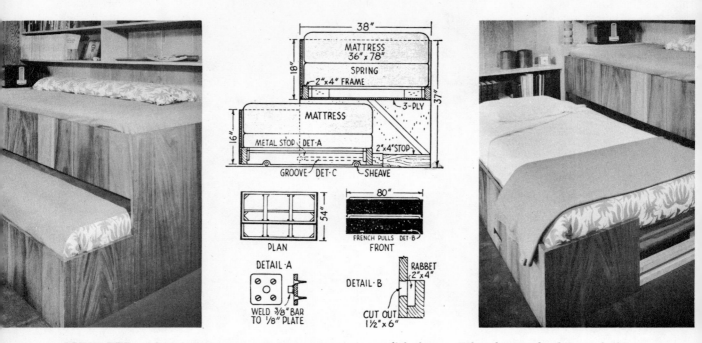

BUNK BED *with stair-step arrangement saves space in small bedroom. When bottom bunk is pushed in, the side of the top bunk becomes a backrest for "sofa." There is plenty of headroom. Architect: Philip Fisk.*

for quick warmth for the bedroom or washroom. For the cabin without running hot water, a stand for a hot tea-kettle near the basin is a "must," and even without regular plumbing, surface drainage can be provided for a standard sink or basin. A marble dresser top, if you can find one, is a sturdy, splash-proof standby to the dressing room equipment.

The bedroom is the logical place to store the items related to that area:

1. Clothing: Family vacation wardrobes should be pro-tected from mildew, rodents and moths and other insects. Assign a special section to heavy work clothing and sports attire where it will not crush or soil other garments, and keep an extra assortment of wraps and bathing suits on hand for guests.

2. Linen and bedding: It is a good idea to line one bunk or closet with metal for permanent storage of all mattresses and blankets. Linens should, of course, be kept near the point of use, and special compartments can often be built under bunks or into headboards for these items.

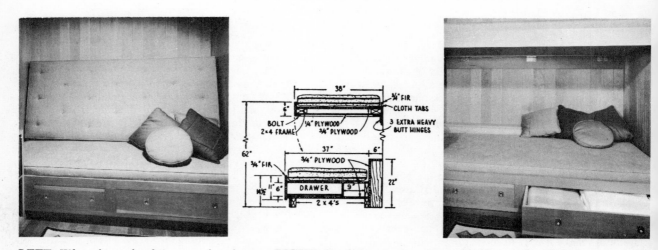

LEFT: *When down, bunk is seven-foot lounge.* **RIGHT:** *Bunk in raised position is held to wall with heavy butt hinges, locked in place by two ¾ by ¾-inch square spring bolts which fit into the wall. Top custom-built mattress is held in place with tabs attached to plywood base. Architect: Joseph Esherick.*

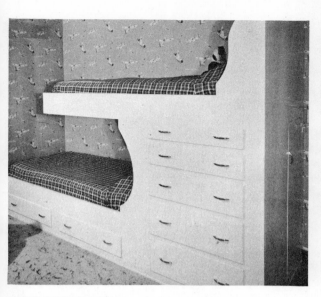

THIS INTERESTING *cantilevered arrangement permits storage in drawers below bunks and in cupboard at head.*

FOUR *bunks under sloping roof that allows ample head-room. Storage includes sleeping-bag rack at far end.*

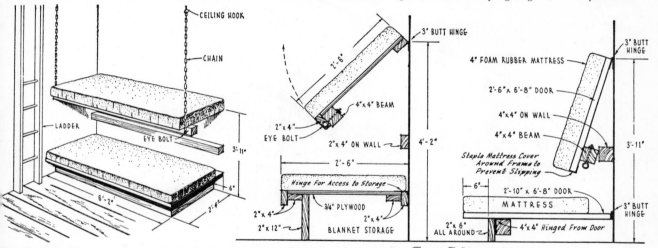

VARIATIONS *on combination fold-down, chain-supported couch-bunk designed by architect Henrik Bull for overflow sleeping in mountain cabin. Fish net stretched from ceiling to edge of top bunk could add safety.*

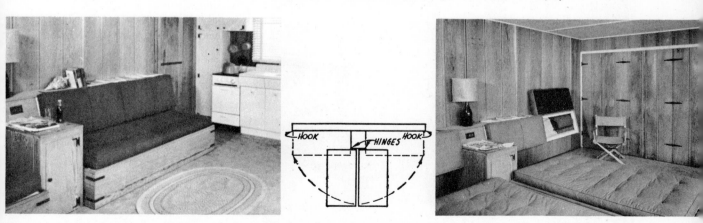

LEFT: *Kitchen alcove is open and beds are in daytime position as sofas; built-in storage cases reduce bed width to comfortable seat width.* **RIGHT:** *Beds swing out for sleeping. Note bedding storage space.*

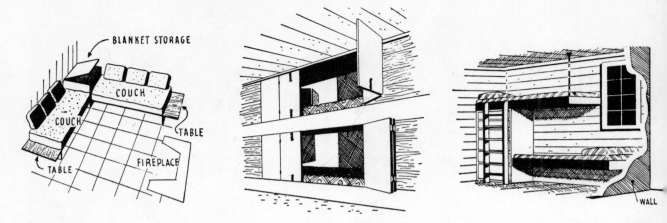

LEFT: *Sofas-by-day, beds by night do double furniture duty but require more space than bunks. Corner blanket storage cabinets serves as night table.* **CENTER:** *Wall bunks can be closed off from living room; give on to the porch.* **RIGHT:** *To eliminate closed-in feeling, stagger lower and upper bunks, add a window.*

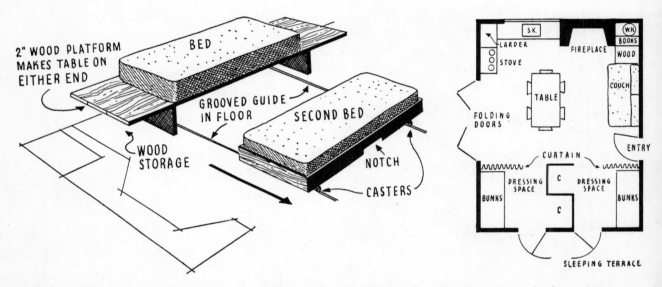

LEFT: *Avoid upper-lower combination with pull-out frame stored under a couch. Extension under base of couch makes "end tables."* **RIGHT:** *In above plan arrangements have been made to sleep five persons (four bunks plus couch) not bad planning when you consider that the size of the cabin is only 18 by 24 feet.*

LEFT: *Hinged bunk saves space but labor involved opening and closing may be a disadvantage.* **CENTER:** *Wall panel forms platform for let-down bed. 2 by 4 frame is bolted to cross pieces of door; springs are bolted to it.* **RIGHT:** *Bunk variation on the two-couch idea, has the advantage of increased storage space.*

ONE-ROOM CABIN *with carefully budgeted space for cooking, sleeping, storage. Cook can visit with guests, but kitchen work counters are screened from view. Ladder leads to extra sleeping area on the balcony.*

Planning the cabin kitchen

The vacationing housewife may be willing to leave her cares behind her, but not her kitchen conveniences. No matter how rustic and informal the rest of the cabin, the kitchen should be as up to date as possible if the cook, too, is to enjoy herself "away from it all."

Gas or electric appliances are, of course, ideal, and compact all-in-one units, including refrigerator, sink, stove and storage are available for the small kitchen.

Be sure of a constant ice supply if an ice box must substitute for a refrigerator—ice houses, stocked during winter months, are located in many northern lake-side regions. Coolers are still popular; but must be located so the air inlet is on the shady side of the cabin. Never store food where animals might get at it.

Without standard utilities, kerosene and butane stoves operate efficiently, and the old-fashioned wood stove is a cabin stand-by. The wood stove with a water reservoir assures a supply of hot water for dishes and washing, eliminating the need for constant kettles atop the stove when there is no other water heater.

Walls and floor around the wood stove should be protected from flying sparks by brick, tin, or asbestos. The woodbox should be located as conveniently as possible to the stove and to the outdoor wood supply.

Where electricity is available, a useful combination is a wood stove for kitchen warmth and general cooking,

plus an electric hot plate or small stove for a small, quick meal or a single pot of coffee. It is handy, particularly on moving day, to bring a complete hot meal to the cabin in an electric roaster. Barbecue cookery also adds variety; in cabin country, douse coals afterward, and take every possible fire precaution.

If kitchen space is small, consider an apartment-size stove (20 inches wide). Under-the-counter refrigerators also save space.

Portable appliances can help make cabin life easy: Electric fry pans, sauce pans, pressure cookers, toasters, griddles, rotisseries. It is a simple matter to bring one or more of them home for a weekend or a vacation.

The vacation larder is often beset to provide impromptu meals for guests of elastic numbers and appetites, and infrequent shopping trips make it necessary to plan carefully for well-rounded menus and convenient storage of staple goods. Canned foods, prepared baking mixes, dried fruits and vegetables will go a long way toward supplementing a few fresh items. A kitchen blackboard facilitates a constant inventory of these supplies, which should be kept in airtight metal or glass containers for maximum protection against rodents and insects.

There are a number of points to consider in the storage of food and utensils:

1. The kitchen and pantry will be overloaded with

SHUTTER DOORS *can be pulled across tiled counter of this compact kitchen. Drawers at end of counter.*

STOVE *in picturesque setting heats dining area, also doubles as a warming oven and handy serving buffet.*

TWO LARGE DOORS *with built-in shelves open off big room, revealing small kitchenette with sink and stove. Shelves are lipped so cans won't fall off.*

more food and possibly even more utensils than are required for an urban family.

2. Storage for heavy sacks of vegetables and cases of canned and bottled goods should be provided near the unloading point.

3. Everyday staples and utensils should be conveniently placed near work centers.

4. A cabin freezer full of food could be a worry during unoccupied periods, especially in mountain areas where electrical power may be uncertain due to storms. There is an easy way to check to be sure that food has not defrosted and perhaps spoiled: Leave an empty jar in the freezer with a funnel in the top, and a couple of ice cubes in the funnel. When you arrive at the cabin look to see whether the ice cubes have melted into the jar. If they are intact, you may be sure there has been no significant defrosting.

Still another consideration of the kitchen area is the arrangement for dining.

Arrange first to make the most of vacation surroundings: to sit near a window overlooking a favorite view, or to enjoy eating near the warmth of the cabin fireplace on chilly evenings.

A table that can be moved about, indoors and out, in keeping with the season and the guest list is so much the better. Tables whose heights and seating capacities can

KITCHEN *in a closet has combination sink, range, refrigerator plus counter. Design: Burde-Shaw-Kearns.*

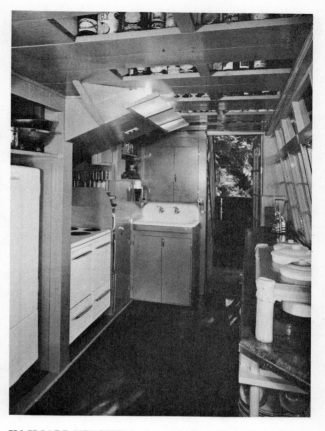

IN SMALL KITCHEN, *the canned goods and staples are stored overhead. Light box illuminates shelves.*

be ingeniously varied add to the cabin's flexibility, but they must be strong and simply constructed to be practical. A sturdy drop leaf design is always dependable.

Some families may prefer a breakfast bar arrangement, particularly when space is at a premium. This fixed counter, which also serves as a low partition and storage unit, can be equipped with blinds or shutters that will completely screen the kitchen area between meals. Stools have become popular for seating, however, it is more pleasant to be able to lean back in a standard chair than to perch atop a high stool, so plan for a comfortable compromise.

For cabin dishes consider plastics, restaurant-weight china or good pottery, and stainless steel utensils. Mugs serve as both glasses and cups, and eliminate saucers. Have plenty of trays on hand.

The dining table, after meals, doubles as a work table, desk, and game center. For this reason, as well as to lighten the vacation laundry load, the surface shoud be sturdy and easily cleaned. Linoleum is a very satisfactory table top, and can be wiped clean and dry in an instant. Natural wood, carefully finished and waxed, can be made to resist heat and stains; and there are many excellent plastic surfaces on the market.

Open shelving for dishes is often attractive but is generally impractical as it means extra work washing dishes that became dusty or dirty during prolonged absence.

COMBINATION *of wood stove and small electric unit provides quick emergency heat plus old-fashioned comfort. Wood storage is under hinged seat (right).*

LEFT: *Pass-through window from kitchen to deck ties interior to outside living areas. Architects Terry and Moore.* **CENTER:** *Cleaning tools, ironing board share left cupboard, canned goods and supplies over hamper in center and washer at right.* **RIGHT:** *Photo shows same area when storage doors are all closed.*

LARGE *storage closet has two bins for vegetables, shelves for staples alongside pots and pans. Door space has been designed for flat pan lids, pie tins.*

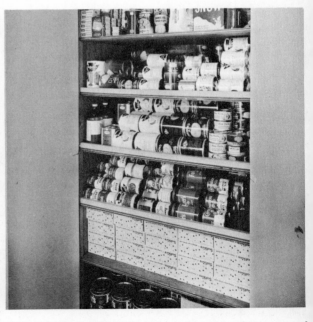

QUANTITY STORAGE *for case lots of food is increased by stacking cans on sides. A lip on the shelves holds cans in. Architects: Hamlin and Martin.*

DINING SHELF *is built at the standard thirty-inch height, affords the maximum enjoyment of the view.*

THREE *hinged panels of free-standing unit will accommodate eight people, fold down to conceal storage.*

SET UP *in the kitchen, this black table top makes an attractive breakfast counter for the cabin.*

CONVENIENT *serving counter is open to kitchen, left photo; can be screened off by Venetian blind (right).*

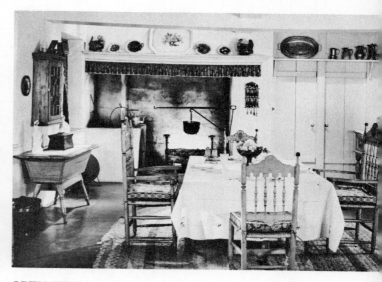

DISAPPEARING *table, 8 feet long, is 2-inch slab of circular-cut oak. Support mounted on wheels.*

OPEN FIRE *provides cheery background for rainy-day meals. Sturdy colonial furniture adds homey touch.*

GRANITE BOULDERS *surround metal fireplace. Seats are also used for sleeping. Design: David Tucker.*

LARGE STONES *face fireplace. Four heat circulating ducts spread heat from front. Note beam mantel.*

Consider a cabin fireplace

A cabin heated by a crackling fire in the fireplace is part of the romance of cabin living. The fireplace grouping, the very heart of the cabin, can be worked out in combination with bookshelves and fireside seats, a cheerful corner for dining and reading, and plenty of space for the tired sportsman to relax in warm, dry comfort.

A rack for wet clothes, a handy supply of wood and perhaps a chopping block on the hearth will save steps.

Numerous arrangements are suggested on these two pages and throughout the book. The *Sunset* book, "How to Design and Build Your Fireplace," suggests more ideas and building techniques.

Today the cabin owner has the choice of a custom built fireplace of brick or stone or a prefabricated metal style. The latter is usually quite simple to install, taking only

one day for anyone with a handyman's bent for that sort of thing.

A circulating type fireplace with a prefabricated metal fire box can be set in the wall just like a regular fireplace, but it has vents that take in cool air and circulate warm air back into the room. Circulating vents are also beneficial in a regular masonry fireplace. (Since a fireplace can seldom perform the heating duties for the whole cabin, auxiliary heaters are usually necessary. See section on Heating.)

Where there is a great distance from ground level to floor level, the cost of a masonry fireplace may be prohibitive.

A fireplace need not be installed when the cabin structure is being built. It is a simple matter, and not too expensive, to frame in for one and add it later.

COPPER *fireplace hangs from masonry chimney, keeps entire cabin warm most months. Design: Alan McRae.*

BRICK *masonry is set in steps, used as stairway to sleeping quarters. Rod above opening for fire screen.*

LARGE *fireplace with handy but handsome firewood storage recess. Design is by Lutah Maria Riggs.*

LEFT: *Economical hood-type fireplace has 12 square feet of reflecting surface. Design: Wendell Lovett.*
CENTER: *Buoy-shaped metal fireplace, in center of room, radiates heat on all sides.* **RIGHT:** *Brick-base fireplace with copper hood and wide metal chimney warms entire room. Design by William F. Hempel.*

Workable ideas

There is an almost endless list of ideas, some novel—some ordinary, that make a cabin a more comfortable place to live.

Furniture that can take it, that can be wiped clean in an instant, is more practical than overstuffed pieces that are inclined to musty mildew and require dry cleaning. Paint and ingenuity will coordinate the unmatched units and contrive space-saving arrangements that serve more than one function. Hutch benches, studio couches, folding tables and chairs all increase cabin flexibility. The handyman can construct sawbuck tables and barrel chairs. Cane chairs of Mexican or Chinese manufacture are well designed and inexpensive.

Denim, burlap, monk's cloth, ticking, sail cloth, canvas, muslin, plastics—these and many other materials are well suited to cabins, being sturdy, practical and casual.

A tool chest fitted with at least an axe, saw, hammer, pliers and wire cutter; and paint, kerosene and stove fuel

WINTER ENTRANCE *is small separate hall, a buffer between outside cold and interior warmth. Boots are scraped on furnace grate over shallow floor well.*

COMBINATION RACK *for water skis and snow skis is shown in the photograph above.*

When skiers become amphibious, their ski storage problem obviously doubles. A family in Redmond, Washington resolved this problem by mounting both water skis and snow skis in racks in a hallway near an outside door.

The water ski rack is 5 feet long. Skis are pushed up into 1 by 7-inch slots in a ¾ by 4-inch plywood bracket on top. To form notches in the 6-inch-wide bottom bracket, two pieces of the same plywood were glued together; the top one has slots cut in it.

The bottom bracket for the snow ski rack is made the same way and is 30 inches long. The top bracket, 4 inches wide, has 3¾-inch notches at 1-inch intervals in the outer edge. Chains, each 4½ inches long, hold the skis in these notches. Each chain is attached to a screw eye at one end and has a hook on the other.

For the family that uses snow skis only, or uses water skis only the above instructions can be modified for that singular purpose.

for your cabin

should be kept in a utility section. Every cabin needs a fire extinguisher and first aid box and instructions for their use should be clearly posted.

Neat racks and compartments are useful for storage of skis, guns, fishing equipment or what-have-you.

Bookcases and breakfast bars are commonly designed with this dual purpose in mind. Window seats with hinged tops double as chests, and many small "extras" may be cached in the shallow space between the studding.

For a cabin located in the snow country, an upstairs entry is a good idea for use when drifts are deep.

Since guests are often invited to the cabin and facilities are limited, a compartmented bath is well worth considering.

Actually camping on the cabin site and making a model of the cabin and what will go in it can avoid mistakes that would go undetected until too late.

ENTRANCE HALL *space next to hot water heater and furnace has built-in closets and shelves, utilizes heat from furnace registers to dry wet clothing.*

TIPPED UP *deck section protects full length glass door and windows from weight of piled up snows and water seepage. Fold section down during the summer.*

CABLE CART *moves supplies down to cabin from road above. Box has wheels, is kept on track by sides of chute. Electric winch at top operates cart.*

INEXPENSIVE ANSWER *to storage problem is series of unfinished pine chests of drawers, uniform in height.*

A GOOD SUBSTITUTE *for a fireplace is an old black pot-bellied stove in a corner setting of used brick.*

HEADBOARD *of bed is hinged at base, lets down for storage of pillow, blanket. Open shelf for books.*

A GLASS *wind-protection fence is a good idea for ocean beach cabins. This one is seven feet high.*

EXTRA BED *folds in the middle for compact storage. Plenty of room also to store bedding in closet.*

THE SPIRAL STAIRWAY *pictured above is especially well suited to a cabin as it takes little space (a 5-foot-diameter stairwell) and is of simple design.*

There are 12 treads that rest on 2 by 2-inch ledgers on 2 by 6 posts. The treads are 30 inches long and 4 inches wide where they notch into the center pole, 16 inches wide at the outer ends.

The peeled log pole's diameter varies from 7 inches at the bottom to 5 inches at the top.

The lower of the two photographs shows the view looking down. The hand "rail" is made of 1-inch manila rope and held in place by brass-plated screw eyes.

CLOSED, *the storage unit shown at top of column becomes a paneled wall by closing the two doors.*

HOW-TO-DO-IT

Practical Planning

The following section is an attempt, not to solve all the questions that arise with becoming a cabin owner, but to raise the questions.

Starting at this end of the chapter and looking toward the finish, the distance appears formidable. Be comforted. Not all of the questions occur for everybody, and most of them are readily solved by professionals.

The major areas are:
- Selecting a site
- Building materials
- Utilities
- Financing
- Fire prevention
- Security
- Access roads
- Pier building
- Water supplies
- Septic tank

Some notes on how to get started in each area follow.

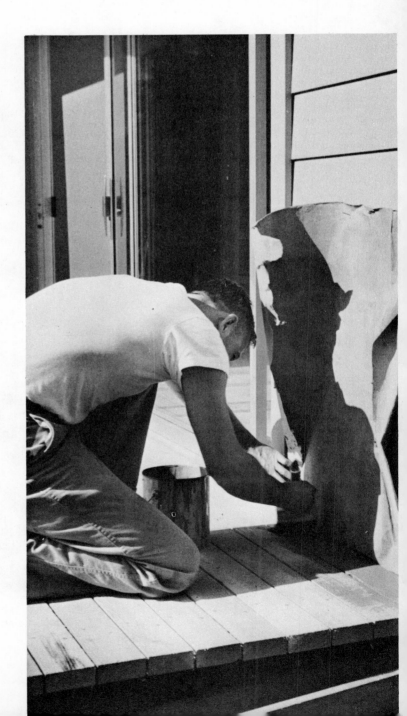

SELECTING A BUILDING SITE

In the great number of cases, the decision to build a cabin or vacation house is made a long time before the prospective builder decides where.

Most owners-to-be know the kind of country where they want to build, and maybe even have a good idea of which town will be the closest, or which river is going to be the source of all future pan-fried trout. Even that much is only the first shot in the battle.

For purposes of discussion, it is best to assume that the start has to be from scratch, and that the process is to be one of elimination.

One way to begin to localize an area is to decide just how many hours' driving you are willing to invest in reaching a leisure retreat. If you plan to visit it weekends throughout much of the year, distance as measured in travel time from home is of considerable importance.

When the limit in time is set, a radius can be marked on a map, and all the possibilities inside it explored.

Local sources of information can be invaluable time savers, both as correspondents and as mines of information.

Letters to local forestry or park officials, to chambers of commerce, and to local real estate agents can reveal much. The primary questions would concern availability of sites, but other points to inquire about would be recreation facilities, access in all seasons, utility districts, contractors, and building material costs.

The county agriculture extension agent will be able to provide weather information from U.S. Department of Agriculture digests.

Once an area begins to sound promising for your particular needs, then a trip to it is the next logical step.

If an area begins to be highly impressive, arrange to stay for several days at least, in order to have time to roam around in it, talking to people, and getting a feel of the place.

Subscribe to the local newspaper.

If, after all of that, its luster is undimmed, it is time to start looking for a lot, undeveloped or with a cabin already on it.

Agencies to Visit

These are some of the agencies.

REAL ESTATE BROKERS

Most beach property and most mountain property in the vicinity of developed ski areas is privately owned, and available either through development corporations or real estate brokers.

Development corporations seem to be growing in number almost weekly in the populous parts of the Western states. Their normal method is to purchase an enormous property, install utilities and roads, and usually some recreational facilities, then to offer sub-divided sites either for sale outright, or on long-term leases. Some of them have committees to impose architectural control.

Some are excellent companies, dedicated to preserving much of the wilderness flavor of a naturally beautiful area. Others seem to have organized themselves solely for the purpose of scraping every vestige of vegetation off the land they control. None are of interest to the seeker of remote solitude, but for persons interested in recreation-oriented communities, such developments are of great value.

LOGGING COMPANIES

Policies on sale or lease of logged-over lands vary widely from company to company. There is an increasing trend toward retention of all lands as tree farming areas, but the firms are worth a check.

Firms can be contacted through a local chamber of commerce.

RAILROAD LANDS

The idea lingers that railroad companies still sell land from the vast rights of way granted them in the early days of the West.

Unfortunately for cabin site hunters, it is not true. Almost all such lands have been withdrawn from sale.

DELINQUENT TAX LANDS

Tax delinquent lands are sold several times each year at open auction in most counties. These auctions are frequently the sources of good sites.

Information is available in several ways. Most direct, contact the county assessor or tax collector at the county seat. These offices maintain lists of tax delinquent lands, with geographic locations. The descriptions are sparse, and sites should be inspected personally.

Announcements of auctions are published as bulletins, and as advertisements in the legal newspaper of the county.

It is necessary to be present at an auction to bid on tax delinquent land.

BUREAU OF LAND MGT.

The Small Tract Act, passed by Congress in 1938 and administered by the Bureau of Land Management, was for years a fertile source of cabin sites. In some areas it continues to be just that. In others, notably Southern California, it will be years before existing claims are sorted out and accepted.

The Small Tract Act allows citizens to select certain lands, up to five acres in size, from public lands, and to settle on them. They aren't free. A site may cost from a few hundred on up to several thousand dollars, depending upon its desirability.

The usual course of events is for a person to find out from a county assessor or the Bureau of Land Management which lands are available.

From these, one is selected, and the potential owner then files an application form, available at the bureau office. Certification depends minimally on a personal visit to the site, or to an area within one mile of it.

If the land has been classified for lease, it can be leased as soon as the application is processed (which may be some time). If it has not been classified, it will have to be before the application is accepted. The bureau is offering no guarantees of speed in this process.

Once the lease is granted, the lessee is free to make the improvements which must be made in three years, after which the site is open to outright purchase.

For more complete information, contact the Bureau of Land Management. Address may be obtained from a county assessor.

NATIONAL FORESTS

National Forests are another former source of cabin sites now filled to capacity by a growing population.

There is only one way to get a cabin site in any of California's National Forests these days. That is to buy the cabin of a person with an existing permit, and get a new permit for that site. The condition prevails generally in the West.

For those who are lucky enough to stumble onto the occasionally available site, here is how the process works:

Sites in National Forests are never sold. The Forest Service awards use permits to individuals; the permits allow the holder to build a cabin on the site.

The original permit-holder can sell his cabin, at which time his permit is cancelled, and a new one issued to the purchaser of the cabin. There is an annual use fee, usually about 5% of the appraised value of the lot.

The Forest Service retains considerable control over the use of the site. Notably, no commercial activity is permitted. No livestock, saddle horses, or poultry can be kept on the site. The premises must be kept in good repair and in orderly condition.

NATIONAL AND STATE PARKS

Cabin sites are not available at all in National Parks at present. Most state parks are also closed to residential building of any sort.

Specific Considerations

Beauty is rampant in the Western wilderness. But, same as with girls, mere beauty is not the whole requirement. Consider:

1. Orientation: How is the lot situated in regard to sun? Is it in the path of, or sheltered from prevailing weather? What about view? Can a cabin be placed to take advantage of morning sun and afternoon shade? How private will it be? Does orientation allow for later expansion of the house? An ideal site would be oriented to get morning sun, afternoon shade (unless it's a ski cabin), and be out of the heaviest storm winds.

2. Utilities: Water is of foremost importance. Check available stream, spring, or well water by having it tested through the county or state department of health. Septic fields should be installed with health department approval. Electric power or natural gas costs should be known, if available. Is other fuel available? If so, at what cost and by what methods of delivery? Is wood available for a fireplace?

3. Weather: In the mountains or by the ocean, weather varies in very short distances. Two sites in the same general area may have widely different microclimates. Mountain and sea winds generally blow up-canyon or away from the sea during the day, down-canyon or toward water during the night. Avoid choosing a natural wind gap as a building site. Such gaps reveal themselves where trees lean away from the wind, and carry most of their foilage on the lee side.

If mosquitoes or other swamp insects are a problem, try to get upwind of them so they get blown into somebody else's territory.

Cold air tends to settle in pockets or depressions. Mountain meadows are often excessively cold at night unless they are open to circulating air.

Off-season weather can be a surprise. Winter snows might be deep enough to keep you away from a cabin for several months. Desert-like summers may afflict a place with delightfully balmy springs. Ocean fogs may prevail all summer at some beaches.

4. Topography: What effect will contour and soil condition have on building and living? How about drainage? Is there a danger of flooding from watershed, stream, or tides? Is the site in the path of a wet season stream? Are slides or snowslides possible? Are overhanging banks or boulders threats? If there is to be a garden, what are the soil conditions? Will future construction block the only good drainage channels? Is the property likely to collect drifting snow? Will sand blow away from beach cabin foundations? Will the soil support a foundation?

5. Accessibility: Is the site uphill or down from the access road? It is ordinarily much easier to transport building materials and cabin supplies down rather than uphill to a site. Can access road and parking area be constructed and maintained? How will supplies be transported into the house? What escape routes are available in case of forest fires? Do you have to obtain access through private property? If the cabin is intended for winter use, how far is it from an all-weather road? Can your own access be kept open in winter? Will roads be passable in wet weather?

6. Construction costs: Check distance at which building materials are available, cost of transportation to site. Are native materials available on the site? How far will it be necessary to transport carpenters or other craftsmen? How much site-clearing will be necessary before building can begin? Will excavation be necessary? At what cost? What road and bridge construction will be needed for access? Will special equipment be required to deal with the site if it is on a hillside or other difficult situation? Must the building be specially designed to withstand heavy snow loads? Will a beach site need a sea wall?

What are local code requirements? Can financing be arranged locally, or in the owner's home city?

7. Maintenance costs: What are insurance rates? What about present or future assessments for roads or utilities? What will maintenance costs be for private roads or trails? How will purely local factors affect upkeep: the corrosive effect of sea air? heavy snow loads? What are opening and closing costs each year for a seasonal cabin? What costs for private police protection?

8. Vegetation: How do present trees affect shade and wind? What trees and other vegetation will have to be removed? Does the plant life of the area conflict with known family allergies? What about poison oak, ragweed, and other polliniferous plants? If you can keep horses or pack animals, what is the availability and cost of grazing and feed?

9. Fauna: What about wild animal life you may want to hunt, or protect? Deer, rabbits, squirrels, waterfowl, shellfish, and fish.

What is the pest population? Deer, bear, rats, porcupines, skunks, mice, snakes.

Are there insect pests locally? Mosquitoes, yellow jackets, ants.

10. Recreational facilities: Do you wish to be near or far, far from dancing, motion picture theaters, community sports, swimming, surfing, boating, hunting, fishing, hiking, mining, rockhounding?

11. Legal responsibilities: Sometimes the purchase or acquisition of rural real estate involves the buyer (or seller) in a tangle of legal complications involving water or mineral rights, or easements. If the lot that interests you is located on a stream, does it affect a long-used spring, or an informal road? It is always prudent to check into established usages.

BUILDING STYLES AND MATERIALS

When both materials and architectural style harmonize with their natural surroundings, they are likely to be the right choices for a cabin.

The following section outlines some of the choices from the ground up, noting limitations and advantages in different kinds of areas from high mountains to low deserts.

Building Materials

Mainly, cabins are built of sturdy, roughly-finished materials.

FOUNDATIONS

At first thought, it would not seem that an unfinished, sometimes-lived-in house needs the same sturdy underpinnings required to hold up a big town house.

But many cabins are on rugged, even precipitous sites. Some are on unstable ground. Most cabins are deliberately put where they take an unmerciful beating from the weather.

In short, cabin foundations ought to be husky. Here is a quick introduction to the commonest types.

Posts: Wood posts are often used to support smaller structures, but they are not generally recommended by building experts. Cedar, locust, redwood, and cypress heartwood can be used without special protection. These woods have tight grain and high resin content, so are resistant to decay and insect attack. Woods impregnated with pentachlorophenol or zinc naphthenate also resist exposure well.

Posts should be a foot or so in diameter, long enough to extend below the frost line in cold country, or, better yet, down to solid rock or dense gravel. A large flat stone is generally placed at the bottom of each post-hole.

Posts are the least dense of all basic foundation materials. They disintegrate more quickly than denser materials, are more susceptible to rot, insects, and other ills. When they have to be bought, they are as expensive as concrete piers in many areas.

The obvious place for posts is on sandy beach sites, where pressure-treated (creosote) pilings are the only way to anchor a place.

Stone: Two large, rather flat boulders laid one atop the other make a common and often serviceable support. Two stones are used because the joint between them stops the rise of moisture and the top stone remains dry. For this reason, the stones should not be cemented or mortared together.

Considerable care should be taken to pair rocks so they fit firmly and evenly together, to prevent slipping or shifting under the building's weight.

This system is best used where the cabin sits on solid or nearly solid rock. Otherwise, it is necessary to dig down to solid rock or firm gravel, and use concrete piers to get up to grade level.

Concrete Piers: Perhaps the commonest cabin foundation is made of a series of concrete piers. Piers can be cast at the site using wood, metal, or building paper forms. If civilization is close enough at hand, it may be less troublesome to buy and haul in pre-cast piers. These are inexpensive and adequate in most parts of the West.

Cabin builders who object to the traditional pier shape can cast cylinders or cones with their own forms.

Concrete dyes can be used to get rid of the ordinary gray of cement where an aesthetic objection occurs.

In cold weather country, piers should extend below the frost line. Regardless of climate, they should rest on solid support.

Piers allow excellent ventilation under a cabin, but they do not keep out rodents or other unwanted beasties. Properly installed, they provide sturdy and long-lasting support for any but extraordinarily large cabins.

Continuous Concrete: Continuous concrete is the most satisfactory and permanent foundation. Weight is evenly distributed, assuring even support for the whole structure.

The rule of thumb requirement for concrete foundations is that they be based on footings which are at least twice as wide as the finished wall. In marshy or unstable soil, an even wider footing may be necessary. Foundation wall width varies according to the weight to be supported. It is a good idea to make walls at least two inches thicker than the logs or timbers to be supported.

Costs of a concrete foundation is determined by availability on the site of usable sand and gravel, transportation costs, type and size of construction, topography and soil characteristics.

In some relatively well-developed areas, pre-mixed concrete can be bought economically.

FLOORS

The problem of whether to have concrete slab or wood flooring can cause the prospective beach or mountain cabin owner a lot of soul-searching and vacillation. Desert cabin owners might think of the slab first and stay with it.

The site and other construction materials to be used may actually make your choice for you.

Concrete slab is easy to pour if the site is fairly level and close to roads, or, better yet, close to a pre-mix plant. It is the best surface on which to lay flagstone, brick, linoleum, or tile floors.

Abundant sand and gravel on the site makes concrete mixing relatively easy. A slab is rodent-free. It helps keep the house close to the ground, making for low, pleasant building lines and ease in landscaping. A slab is easier to clean than a wood floor.

If the site is well drained it is not necessary to use a waterproof membrane in slab construction (see the sketches). Unless soil is rocky, a foot of crushed rock or gravel under the slab will help keep it dry.

Site and other problems may eliminate a slab. Cost of transporting cement to a remote site may be prohibitive. Excavation necessary for slab installation may come too high, or be impossible. Absence of usable sand and gravel often eliminates use of a slab in isolated areas. Sea beach sand and gravel are unusable because their high salt content interferes with proper bonding of the elements in the mix.

Steep slopes and rocky or adobe soils are against slab construction. Where the ground freezes, slabs tend to buckle and disintegrate under the constant and extreme expansion and contraction caused by temperature changes. Unstable soils or adobe can have almost as disastrous an effect on a slab.

Wood floors are in general more aesthetically complementary to log or other rough-textured cabin construction.

TWO FLAT ROCKS. *Good foundation except in cold country. Dry joint blocks rise of moisture.*

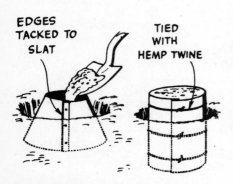

PIER FORMS *can be adapted to avoid traditional shape. Piers must rest in concrete pads.*

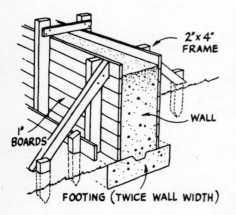

CONTINUOUS CONCRETE *is sturdiest, longest-lasting of all foundations. It distributes weight best.*

In cabin areas, there are often saw mills where rough lumber and delivery service are available at low cost.

Given weathertight construction, wood floors are ordinarily warmer to the touch than concrete. Wood is a less effective heat conductor than concrete, a boon in cold-night climes.

Wood floors can be made of almost any rough or finished lumber, depending on availability and the degree of finish desired. Tongue and groove 2 by 6 boards make a very weathertight floor. They are particularly effective where no subflooring is to be put down.

If a cabin or beach house site permits the use of either wood or concrete, and neither choice has especially strong appeal, it may be best to talk to people who have been living in the area for some time. Any site has its own special problems, but the experience of others under roughly similar conditions can reveal some factors that do not show on the surface.

If standard materials do not answer your floor problems, or if you are of an especially experimental turn of mind, all of the following possibilities have been used on one or more occasions: asphalt, asphalt-cement compound, concrete or lightweight aggregate blocks, exterior grade plywood, compressed sawdust, panels, wood blocks on packed earth, and earth packed hard and stabilized with an asphalt compound.

MASONRY WALLS

Masonry, like any other basic building method, has advantages and disadvantages, proponents and detractors.

On the plus side: No great skill is needed to erect a rough masonry wall for a mountain or beach cabin. The difference between one and four walls is time.

Once erected, a masonry wall is impervious to termites, rats, or other pests. Weather, even bitter cold and deep snow, is no match for good masonry construction.

Site materials often can be used for adobe or stone construction. Cabins built of site materials tend to fit most harmoniously into their native surrounds.

The man who does his own work lowers the cash cost of his cabin considerably.

Fire risk is low in a masonry structure, a fact which is reflected in fire insurance rates.

On the negative side: Work goes slowly, especially if an amateur mason does his own. It is tough, heavy physical labor.

Most masonry construction requires heavier foundations and footings than a frame building does. Erecting a masonry building at an isolated site may pose problems of transportation for steel reinforcement, concrete, and other materials.

A botched job tends to be a durable and even permanent blight on the landscape, and a wretched monument to its builder's mistakes.

Earthquakes require extra reinforcement in many parts of the West.

The following types of masonry walls are within reach of most Westerners who have enough confidence in their building skills to consider doing much or all of their own work.

Stone: Bearing walls of stone require a full concrete or rock foundation. Walls will, of course, be extra heavy, so footings as well as foundation walls should be proportionately thicker and wider than for wood structures.

Stone walls ordinarily should be at least 18 inches thick at the bottom, and taper to 8.

The thickness at the base means the foundation has to be 20 inches wide, and the footing 40 inches.

There are two basic types of stone work, rubble (uncut stones) and ashlar (cut).

Ashlar is expensive enough that most cabins are of uncut stone. Working with uncut stone is more difficult, both from a structural and design point of view.

In choosing stones, or checking to see that an adequate supply is available, keep in mind the scale of the finished house and choose sizes accordingly. A good rule to follow is that the face area of the largest stones laid should not be more than five times the face area of the smallest ones.

A man who built his own stone-walled house offered these further hints for pleasing appearance: Set each stone in a horizontal position, using stones with long, thin proportions. Use several different kinds of stones to give the wall variety in color and texture. However, exercise these freedoms within limits. Stones of intense colors seldom look at home in a wall that is predominantly of medium grays and browns. Small stones tend to look fussy if numerous. Oddly shaped stones of any size tend to disturb the serene balance of horizontal stones.

His working routine was simple and effective. Gathered stones were separated into three stacks. Stack one was of properly shaped and attractive stones. Stack two was of similarly shaped but less appealing stones. Stack three was of small, sharp-edged stones to use as chinking.

All stones were brushed clean to assure good bond with the mortar, and were kept cool and damp so they would not dry the mortar too fast.

The trowel was small, a five-incher, because it was most maneuverable working with irregular surfaces.

Mortar was applied with a lavish hand so each stone could be nestled by joggling it into its best fit. The joints were raked on the following day, a half-inch deep. Later the interior wall was scrubbed with a 10 percent solution of muriatic acid to get rid of mortar stains. The exterior walls were left to weather.

Where stones are scarce and concrete plentiful, people who enjoy the quality of stone sometimes choose a Flagg masonry wall, a concrete wall faced with cut natural stone. Such walls have to be built with full forms on each side.

Concrete or Aggregate Blocks: Blocks or bricks of regular concrete or one of the lightweight aggregates are in most cases more plausibly built vacation home walls than natural stone ones. They are also more satisfactory than poured concrete, requiring less machinery and no complex forms.

Ordinary blocks are dense and heavy. The lightweight blocks use porous minerals in place of the usual sand, and are often light enough for their larger blocks to be lifted easily with one hand. These lighter blocks, because of their porosity, are better insulators than the regular ones.

All blocks are unusually strong individually, but in walls they require careful reinforcing with steel bars to be safe. Codes are explicit in most areas.

Blocks come in many sizes (commonest of them being 8 by 8 by 16 inches), and in special shapes for corners, ends, partitions, door jambs, joists, window sashes, and the like.

As in the case of stone, a heavy footing is required. Most normal requirements are met by footings as deep as the foundation (which is to say the first course of the wall) is wide, and about eight inches wider than the wall. Unstable soil or marsh conditions require the advice of an engineer.

Concrete blocks are easy for an amateur to handle. If the color is objectionable, they can be painted.

Costs are relatively low, unless long distance drayage charges enter into the picture.

Adobe: A contractor-built adobe can be little more expensive than a frame structure. If you do your own work, the cash cost can be genuinely low.

There's a big if.

The cabin site has to be close to one of a very few adobe manufacturers, and the site has to be open enough so the bricks can be delivered within a very few feet of where the wall is to be erected.

Adobe bricks are several times the size of regular bricks, typically 4 by 8 by 16 inches. They weigh in at 30 pounds apiece, which is why they have to be delivered close to where they are going to be used.

Walls go up rapidly for as long as the builder's arms hold out, but at least the bricks are indestructible, allowing long periods of recuperation if need be.

Principal ingredients are soil, water, and a stabilizing waterproofing agent, usually an emulsified asphalt. Any soil will do that will bake. An ironic exception is "adobe" which will not bake without cracking.

Adobe has some basic structural limitations. Critical formulae govern wall height in proportion to wall thickness, length of single unsupported walls, spacing of openings in the wall, and ratio of open space to total wall surface.

Its advantages are iron durability, excellent insulation, and rugged handsomeness.

It is possible, in the absence of manufacturers, to make your own bricks. All it takes is strength, a talent for mixing the ingredients, and a patience that cannot be exhausted by normal mortal trial. The bricks are fashioned in simple molds, and sun-dried. The curing takes 60 to 90 days.

LOG, CRIB CONSTRUCTION

Most people who think of building a mountain cabin think first of building a log cabin. The cozy log cabin in the woods has strong romantic and historical appeal.

There are complications when matters get down to practical application.

Buying logs is expensive. Skilled workmen are hard to find. Even the required tools are hard to locate.

There are two styles of log construc-

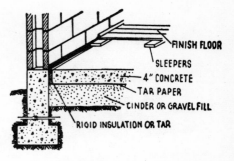

SLAB FLOORS *in most areas must have a waterproof membrane to function properly.*

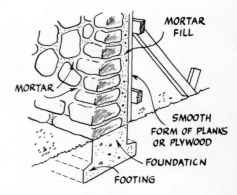

STONE MASONRY *walls can be faced with mortar on inside, or can be doubled so stone faces both ways.*

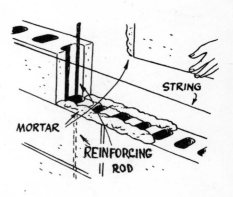

BLOCK MASONRY *walls go up fairly quickly even in amateur hands. They are not always appropriate.*

LOGS CUPPED AND
NOTCHED TO FIT EXACTLY

LOG EDGES SMOOTHED FOR
TIGHT FIT

STANDARD LOG *construction is strong, but difficult. Some pre-cut logs are easy to use.*

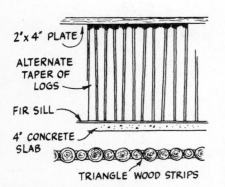

2' x 4' PLATE

ALTERNATE TAPER OF LOGS

FIR SILL

4' CONCRETE SLAB

TRIANGLE WOOD STRIPS

STOCKADE CONSTRUCTION *requires less skill with logs, but lacks strength of diagonal bracing.*

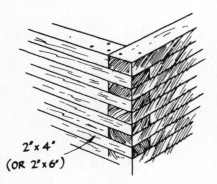

2' x 4'
(OR 2' x 6')

CRIB CONSTRUCTION *has same strength as standard log, but milled lumber fits easily.*

tion, the traditional kind with the logs laid horizontally, and stockade construction, in which logs or half logs are placed upright. The easier style is stockade, since skilled axe work is not required for notching log ends, and smaller logs can be used since their structural function is merely as a curtain wall inside a timber frame.

Logs are not often available at this point in time, at least not merely at the cost of felling nearby trees. Sometimes they can be obtained for a nominal stumpage fee when someone in the area is looking to have property cleared. Sometimes they can be purchased from a public utility company with a supply of power-line poles.

The most likely source is through one of several pre-fab companies which offer specially prepared logs either in prefab kits or in lots of certain sizes. Their great advantage is that they are milled to fit snugly against each other, and they have mill-notched ends. All of this is at the price of the rough rusticity of logs straight from the wood.

Crib Construction is much like log construction in effect. It utilizes 2 by 4 or 2 by 6 inch lumber laid face to face, with each "course" nailed securely to the one below. Corners are cross-lapped (without having to be notched) as the sketch below shows.

Resulting walls are strong and fire-resistant (crib construction is much used by industrial concerns for fire walls).

As with logs, vertical framing is eliminated. The inside surface can be the finished wall.

Mill ends and other odd lengths of relatively low-grade, low-cost lumber can be used.

WOOD FRAME WALLS

Perhaps the greatest single advantage of frame construction is its inherent versatility. It can be what the owner wills, from simplest fishing shack to luxurious ski cabin.

The essential details of each building might be the same: time-honored stud walls sheathed and sided with one of several materials.

Several variations on the stud wall exist, most of them hybridizations with post-and-beam techniques.

All of the following materials work with any of the framing methods.

Unfinished Lumber: Rough sawn lumber is easy for the amateur to use. Applied board-and-batten or lapped, it

makes handsome and serviceable walls. Board-and-batten construction is probably the easier of the two for an amateur. In lightweight structures elaborate wall framing is unnecessary because the vertical boards and battens form a relatively strong bearing wall.

Rough-sawn broad boards or planks are used. A strip of batten is nailed flat over each joint between the broad boards. Specially milled battens have grooves into which the broad boards fit.

Rough boards can be lapped horizontally, shingle-fashion, to create a rugged, durable wall. To strengthen this type of construction, many builders apply sheathing over the frame before lap-siding is applied.

If your building site is in a wooded part of the West, you may be able to buy rough lumber direct from a mill. Lumber purchased at the mill is less costly than it would be at a lumber yard. Some mills even haul.

Milled sidings: Something like 200 different sizes and styles of wood siding are milled in the West. Any well-stocked lumber yard will have several dozen types in stock.

Milled sidings are usually lapped over sheathing, and on houses in sizable colonies. They are a bit too tailored to look at home in anything like natural forest.

Shingles and Shakes: Western cedar, redwood, and cypress shingles and shakes can be used for siding on beach or mountain cabins.

Both shingles and shakes are easy to apply, long lasting, easy to stain, and are almost universally obtainable. Shingled walls, when laid properly, give more insulation than board siding.

When used on side walls, shingles or shakes can have more area exposed to the weather than when they are used as roofing. On a roof, 16-inch shingles are usually laid 5 inches to the weather. On walls, 6 or 6½ inches can be exposed.

Plywood: Where materials have to be hauled long distances to a remote site, plywood can be the most practical of all sidings.

Exterior plywoods are now very durable in severe weather, especially if the edges are protected. Batten strips nailed over the joints can be made to look attractive, even as they protect. (See pages 20-21 for a similar idea.)

Plywood should be thoroughly primed, sealed, and painted, including all edges.

Specialty Sidings: Many large lumber dealers offer rounded siding that gives the effect of debarked half logs, or square-faced timbers chipped to resemble adze-hewn planking. These specialty items are milled with tongue-and-groove and shiplap edges. They go up pretty much like regular siding, except that they are heavier to handle. Most of them are 5¼ to 8 inches wide, and 1 to 3 inches thick.

Where logs are scarce, they are often cheaper than the real thing.

ROOFING

Beach house roofs can be of any material not subject to the corroding effects of salt sea air.

In hot areas, reflective roofing is an advantage. Crushed dolomite over built-up tar and gravel is one answer. Painted canvas is another.

In heavy snow areas, aesthetics sometimes are sacrificed for the extra strength offered by sheet metal or metal shingles.

Most cabin roofs are of shingles or shakes, or of camouflage-colored composition shingles or rolls.

Design for Strength

The U.S. Forest Service once was plagued by collapsing cabins. The causes were lack of diagonal wall bracing, inadequate foundations, lack of trussing joists and rafters, and skimping on nails or bolts.

At length, the Service issued a formal set of requirements, called "Specifications for Buildings in Regions of Deep Snow." Although there is an at least temporary halt to cabin-building in National Forests, the guides are still very useful to anyone planning a cabin that is going to want to be sturdy.

Here are the rules, verbatim.

"The following minimum requirements are recommended for one-story structures:

"In post and girder construction, supporting posts should be 4 by 4 inches spaced not more than 7 feet apart in any direction and should rest on concrete or stone blocks 12 inches square. Girders should be 4 by 6 inches. Continuous footings are recommended for outside walls. Floor joists should be not less than 2 by 6 inches spaced not more than 2 feet on centers. All the above requirements also apply to open porches.

"Studding in outside walls having vertical siding should be 2 by 4 inches spaced 4 feet apart. One 2 by 4 (girt)

must be placed around the building, horizontally, half way between the 2 by 4-inch floor plate and the two 2 by 4-inch ceiling plates. There should then be continuous 2 by 4-inch diagonal bracing running at 45° in each direction between top and bottom plates.

"Where horizontal siding is used, studs should be 2 by 4-inch not more than 2 feet on centers, with top and bottom plates. Diagonally brace between studs at all wall corners.

"Headers over all openings should be *doubled* and proper beams or bridging should be installed on openings over 3 feet wide.

"All roof rafters must be trussed with ceiling joist. Provide vertical bracing at center and diagonal bracing from center at joist to midpoint of each rafter. This bracing must be well spiked. The connections between rafters and ceiling joist must be well spiked or bolted for spans under 12 feet and must be bolted with not less than 2 bolts per joint for spans 12 to 16 feet and with 3 bolts or more for spans 16 to 20 feet, or equivalent connectors shall be used.

"Rafters should be not less than 2 by 6 inches and be spaced not more than 16 inches on center.

"Ceiling joist should be 2 by 6 inches spaced same as rafters.

"Trussed rafters and ceiling joists shall be well spiked to wall plates.

"Joints of low pitched roofs must be made stronger than those of steep pitched roofs for the same snow load.

"Foundations should be of stone or concrete. Wood should not be used for foundation material."

FOR STRONG APPEARANCE

The U.S. Forest Service was also eager to help maintain an atmosphere of natural woodland through careful control of exterior appearance of cabins in National Forest lands. The suggestions of the Service toward this end still have validity. (Granted, there is always room for argument in questions of aesthetics, but at the very least the points are all raised in the list.)

Building design: Generally, cabins fit the ground more readily when horizontal lines predominate and building outlines are low and sprawling.

Wall and Roof Materials: Cabins are fundamentally rustic vacation homes and should present that effect when completed. Rough wood and stone are considered the best basic materials. They harmonize easily with surround-

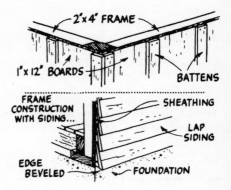

BOARD AND BATTEN *construction goes easily for amateur builder, yet produces strong walls.*

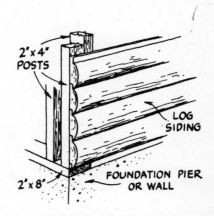

SPECIALTY SIDINGS *offer a useful compromise between natural materials and milled lumber.*

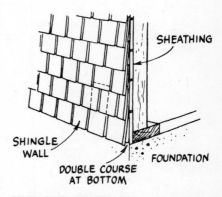

SHINGLE OR SHAKE *walls are good insulators. Walls require fewer shakes than do roofs.*

ings, have a long life with minimum maintenance. Smooth-surfaced and thin materials, on the other hand, look manufactured and lack the strong, rugged appearance necessary in most mountain sites. Approved materials are: peeled logs, hewn logs, log siding, rough sawn lumber, wood shingles, shakes, shingle-tile, composition shingles, and stone. Concrete, masonry blocks, and brick may be used in portions of the exterior in combination with more natural

and rustic materials, providing over-all design is rustic. Smooth or finished lumber may be used for trim and minor areas of the exterior when the basic exterior material is of rougher or more natural stuffs.

Sheet metal, stucco, cobblestones, flexible paper, or felt materials, composition wall materials, and mechanically-laid masonry are classified "undesirable" because of un-natural color, texture, or unsatisfactory performance

against the rigors of mountain winters.

Roofs, too, are required to be of rough-textured materials. Exceptions are when a flat or low-pitched roof is used, little of which is visible from the surrounding ground. Built-up tar and gravel, painted sheet metal and other similar materials may then be used.

Design details: Foundation should be as low as possible consistent with good construction. Use of masonry, concrete or concrete blocks is approved. Pier

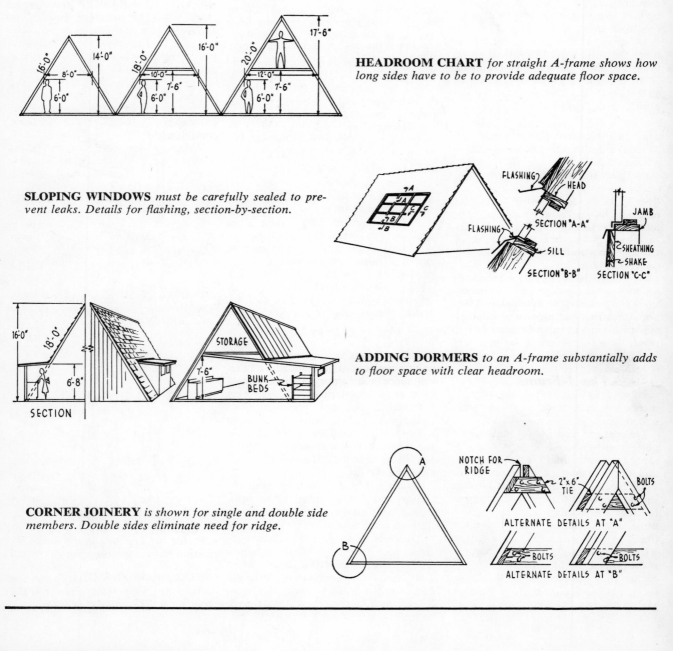

HEADROOM CHART *for straight A-frame shows how long sides have to be to provide adequate floor space.*

SLOPING WINDOWS *must be carefully sealed to prevent leaks. Details for flashing, section-by-section.*

ADDING DORMERS *to an A-frame substantially adds to floor space with clear headroom.*

CORNER JOINERY *is shown for single and double side members. Double sides eliminate need for ridge.*

construction must include siding or heavy lattice-work which extends to ground level to enclose the underpinning.

Windows and doors should be of uniform size and shape. Top or head-level should be at uniform height above the floor. Window area must assure adequate indoor light.

Chimneys and fireplaces are required to be of safe, substantial construction with a solid masonry or concrete foundation. Flue lining is necessary.

Exterior color: Colors generally found in the soil or the bark and foliage of trees are recommended: subdued red, gray, gray-green, or warm brown. Stain or paint may be used, or exterior walls and roof can be left to weather naturally.

Doors and trim may be painted lighter or darker shades of basic colors. Bright colors may be used for small exterior areas, including doors.

Administration of Standards: It isn't to worry, unless you chance upon a cabin in a National Forest when the owner decides to sell. The point of the rule was that allowances could be made where conditions demanded. As examples, sheet metal roofs were sometimes recommended in areas of high fire hazard, or exceptionally heavy snowfall. What the rule used to say was, "When otherwise inappropriate materials are allowed, they must be painted an appropriate color."

The man who wrote that must have had park service green or O.D. in mind. But the point is well taken that a tin roof looks more at ease in a wooded area if it is painted an unobtrusive color.

The A-Frame

The triangular framework, the shape of the simple tent, was one of the first man used for shelter.

It is a self-bracing form that requires a minimum of joinery, and lends itself to one-man construction.

It strikes a responsive chord in the modern Westerner. In fact, the chord gets struck pretty often. The A-Frame is one of the most popular basic styles of construction known in the region.

Advantages: Simple, easy construction is the primary one. The main frames can be formed on the ground. Once the frames are raised, the sheath-ing is both roof and walls, and the outside sheathing can be the interior finish as well.

The A is especially valuable in gaining a sense of space in a small building. With 16-foot sides, the roof peak is about 14 feet above the floor. A rectangular room of the same floor space will seem much smaller with an eight-foot ceiling.

Decks can be added very easily to the A-frame, which normally is built up from a platform anyway. This is an advantage of large dimension in precipitous country where outdoor lounging room is at a premium.

The shape lends itself to a very low-cost mezzanine-type second floor where extra sleeping space can be located.

Disadvantages: The most troublesome problem is the lost spaces near the edges of the floor. This can be alleviated with dormers, or with curved beams, as shown on page 7. Even with these modifications, it is necessary to put furniture and storage on the edges, and keep bare-headed traffic moving in the middle.

Ductwork, pipes, and wiring can be run along the margins of the floor, too.

Doors or windows cut into a sloping wall tend to leak, unless the installation is made with care. Intense light from end walls almost always has to be balanced with light from the center, or else the center of the building tends to be gloomily dark. Skylights may be better than low windows, provided the weather permits them.

Doors cut into a sloping roof have to swing out, against gravity, or have to be set in dormers.

Most cabin builders these days put all doors and windows in vertical walls. They modify the simple tent so it becomes two intersecting tents, or else modify one side to gain added vertical wall space. (See page 68 for a canny engineering job of this sort.)

Equilateral triangles have several favorable aspects to recommend them to amateur builders. All angles are 60°. All members are the same length. The balance between headroom and roof height is automatic. The major decision is how long to make the sides. The accompanying scale sketches should help a beginning planner in his deliberations.

Insulation

A great many cabins are built in areas with rigorous climates, and very few have full-fledged furnaces in them.

People who don't insulate their cabins usually wish they did the first morning they have to set foot on a genuinely frosty floor.

Engineers for utilities companies do not prefer one insulation over another necessarily. Most agree that where cold is the primary factor, glass-fibre mineral wool is efficient. In general, they give batt a slight edge over loose-fill with this type.

A-frame buildings are difficult to insulate because they are all roof. When covered with snow, the heat loss is indeed great. Batt insulation cannot always be installed in an A-frame without ruining the appearance of the interior. In these cases, engineers suggest a layer of 2-inch thick fibreboard underlaying a roof of tar and gravel over 2-inch redwood tongue-and-groove planking. The heat loss without the fibreboard is .32 Btu per hour per square foot per degree of temperature difference from outdoors to indoors. With the insulation, the loss is only .11 Btu under the same conditions.

Where mineral wool batts can be installed, their effects are as follows, according to the calculations of one expert from a utility company:

(The assumptions are 1,300 sq. ft. in the building, a glass to wall ratio of 1 to 4, and a 40° difference in temperature —conditions which would lead to a heat loss of 75,110 Btu per hour in an uninsulated building of this description.)

| Mass Insulation Added | | | |
Ceiling	Wall	Floor	Savings*
4"	0"	0"	32 %
6	0	0	33.2
4	2	0	44.3
4	0	2	46.8
4	4	0	45.3
4	2	2	58.8
4	4	4	61.2
6	4	2	62.3

*In equipment size, operating cost. For example, to maintain the temperature difference of 40°, with no insulation the power requirement would be 22 KW; with four inches of insulation in the ceiling, the requirement would be 15 KW; for the maximum amount of insulation shown, the requirement would be 8.4 KW.

Reflecting insulation seems to be the most effective where over-hot is the problem, rather than super-chilled.

USEFUL ADDRESSES

Some of the following addresses may prove very useful during the planning stages of a cabin.

UTILITY COMPANIES

Inquiries addressed to the Customer Relations Departments of these utility companies will produce good answers to specific questions about availability of service in certain areas, rates, and probable consumption under local conditions.

California Liquid Gas Corp.
Box 5073
Sacramento, Cal. 95817

Pacific Gas & Electric Co.
Room 438, 245 Market Street
San Francisco, Cal. 94106

Puget Sound Power & Light
Bellevue, Wash. 98004

Southern California Edison Co.
P. O. Box 351
Los Angeles, Cal. 90053

STOCK PLANS

The pre-fab and pre-cut manufacturers listed on pages 80-83 offer dozens of fine house plans, some of them in booklet form, and the materials to go with them. The following organizations offer only the plans, not the materials.

American Plywood Association
1119 "A" Street
Tacoma, Wash. 98401

California Redwood Association
617 Montgomery Street
San Francisco, Cal. 94111

Simpson Lumber Company
2000 Washington Building
Seattle, Wash. 98101

Western Wood Products Association
Yeon Building
Portland, Oreg. 97204

Cooperative Farm Building Plan Exchange,
U. S. Department of Agriculture
Beltsville, Md.
or:
Extension Agricultural Engineer
Oregon State University
Corvallis, Oreg.

These last two named organizations have collected dozens of thoughtful cabin designs in the process of gathering good farm building ideas from across the country. The designs are plain, sturdy, and inexpensive.

BUREAU OF LAND MGT.

This is the agency which handles all petitions for sites under the Small Tract Act (see page 101). Inquiries should be addressed to: Bureau of Land Management, with the office address of the state in which you wish to claim a parcel.

Federal Building, Room 3022
Phoenix, Ariz. 85025

Federal Building, Room 4017
650 Capitol Mall
Sacramento, Cal. 95814

667 Insurance Exchange Building
910 - 15th Street
Denver, Colo. 80202

P. O. Box 2237
Boise, Ida. 83701

1245 North 29th Street
Billings, Mont. 59101

P. O. Box 1551
Reno, Nev. 89505

P. O. Box 1449
Santa Fe, N. M., 87501

710 Northeast Holladay
Portland, Oreg. 97232
(office serves Washington)

P. O. Box 11505
Salt Lake City, Utah, 84111

2002 Capitol Avenue
Cheyenne, Wyo. 82001

PLANNING CABIN UTILITIES

Heating and lighting a cabin, and providing an efficient kitchen, may seem puzzling in the absence of a familiar urban environment.

In fact, the whole approach to utilities is about the same wherever a house may be. The cabin gets along with fewer frills. Its equipment is selected with a thought toward long periods of absence. In the case of big snow country, the cabin owner may be in need of an auxiliary power supply for the inevitable outage that follows one or another of the winter's storms. Beyond those differences, however, the amounts or types of utility installations are much alike between home and cabin.

It is fairly likely that a cabin will need both electricity and either natural or liquid petroleum gas. How much of which and for what purpose will be governed by location and availability. The following rough guidelines might serve as a starting point for planning.

Electricity

It would be a rare achievement to find a good cabin site beyond the reach of electric power in this age.

Where electric power is available at reasonable installation and operating costs, it is versatile and safe for every purpose. Utility company experts recommend that the cabin be wired for 240 volts, with at least enough circuits to handle heating, lights, a water heater, and a flock of small appliances. Such a system may never be used to its capacity, but installation cost wouldn't be much less for a minimum capacity that would fall short of later needs.

Heating units in both high mountain and beach areas have to combat moisture as much as cold. Consultants in the Pacific Northwest and northern California both suggest wall-mounted baseboard heaters as the most efficient electric units in current use for these conditions.

The reasoning is that air cools close to the walls, and sinks down them. The long baseboard units warm the air as it passes, before it circulates across the floor area.

In the same connection, many experts recommend models with low wattage per lineal foot—about 225 watts per foot being the consensus.

Shorter, higher watts-per-foot models do not give as even a flow of heat over a wide area.

Utilities company advisers in desert or other hot summer vacation areas recommend the electric heat pump as the best solution because it can both warm and cool an interior. Heat pumps range in size from small, room-sized units to large units with ductwork carrying forced air all through a building.

The same advisers do not recommend portable space heaters anywhere except in uninsulated cabins without fireplaces to toast the huddled inhabitants. Among their disadvantages: They aren't usable when they would help most, during outages.

The primary advantage of any permanent, thermostat-controlled electric unit is that it can be left on during a long absence, set just high enough to keep the building dry and, in mountains, free of frost.

The wisdom of choosing an electric stove depends fairly directly on the location of the cabin and its use. Beach or lowland cabins will have a dependable source of heat for cooking from an electric stove. So will high mountain cabins that are used in summers. Ski cabins are something else. Utilities companies assume at least one major outage per winter for any trunk line. Some recommend straight out the installation of a natural gas or liquid petroleum gas stove. Others recommend an electric stove (especially if that is what the cook is used to back home), with a Coleman camp stove or a similar stove as a stand-by.

Stove or no, the kitchen circuits should be adequate in size and number of outlets to accommodate a toaster, a mixer or blender, and an electric skillet.

Refrigerators and hot water heaters fall into the same area of consideration as the stove.

Lighting belongs indisputably to electricity, in quality at least, wherever possible. In remote areas, some stand-by lights of brighter mien than candles are in order. These stand-by lamps, usually gas lanterns, should be located along the walls rather than in the center of a room. They work better with the walls as reflecting agents, and they permit work to go on in the kitchen without having the cook always struggling with his or her own shadow.

Natural Gas

Natural gas companies are still struggling with the consumer's deeply implanted idea that it isn't safe to go off and leave any gas appliance alone unless it has been shut down completely, pilot and all.

It is no longer true. American Gas Association-approved appliances have safety shut downs that are 100 per cent effective.

So long as they are properly vented, these appliances are safe even if a pilot is extinguished.

In a great many areas in the West, natural gas is just as available as electricity, at competitive prices. Where this is so, the choice of many appliances is purely a personal one. Heat may best be electric where moisture is a difficulty, as noted above. But the rest of the choices—including water heaters, refrigerators, stoves, and even driers—are even-up at worst. In areas of howling storms and heavy snows, they may even have a slight edge in that the pipes are underground and beyond any danger of power failure.

Experts do recommend that gas water heaters be shut off during absences.

Installation of lines and appliances should be done by a plumber. Many utilities companies will recommend reliable men. No utility can connect service until the work is ok'd by a building department inspector.

Liquid Petroleum

LP Gas is a traditional part of cabin life in the United States, largely because it can go anywhere. As one representative says of it, it comes either "in the form of bulk delivery to a storage tank, or, for smaller consumption, exchange cylinders of fuel. We have, on occasion, delivered fuel by dog sled, by ski lift, and by boat."

Gas will do the whole job of heating a cabin and running all kitchen appliances.

In this situation, the cabin-owner leases a tank from the supplier and purchases fuel either on a gallonage basis as delivered, or on a metered basis as consumed (the latter usually when several cabins share a large central tank).

One supplier estimates that a family of four in a 1,000-sq. ft. cabin with good insulation will use 5 to 15 gallons of gas on a weekend for heater, stove, water heater, and refrigerator. The heater is the major variable. Its consumption can range from 2 to 10 gallons.

LP gas works in the same appliances as does natural gas. It burns hotter.

Its main disabilities in comparison with natural gas are two. First, it has to be delivered in most cases. Second, all appliances have to be shut down completely during any prolonged absence of owners from a cabin. Usually, the supply is closed off by a valve at the tank. This means that a competent gas serviceman has to come to light all the pilots on the return of the owners to the cabin.

Most cabin owners in remote areas find LP gas a worthy addition to their power supplies, in an auxiliary role if not in the primary one.

Emergency Power

Whatever the general utility arrangements, it is wise to have some source of portable or auxiliary power in a cabin. The more remote the cabin, the more pressing the need.

There are a few cabins with no other power than that generated by a portable unit.

These are some of the current choices.

An alternator-generator of the type shown in the sketch is compact enough to be carried in a car, yet powerful enough (1,250 watts on a 110-volt alternating current) to supply power for construction tools, or lights, or a refrigerator and some small appliances. It has a permanent-magnet alternator instead of the usual generator with brushes, and is powered by a one-cylinder gas engine. The unit is enclosed in glass fiber for quiet operation, weighs 75 pounds, and costs about $300.

The engine of the other generator shown burns liquid petroleum gas. Advantages claimed for LP gas are longer engine life, lower fuel costs, and no deterioration or difficult starting (as occurs with gasoline) when left unused for months at a time.

These larger generators are available in several sizes from a 2,500-watt home model (shown), costing $540 with remote starting, to a 100-kilowatt generator which is large enough to furnish electricity for a small community.

The converter-charger shown in the drawing is an entirely different source

ALTERNATOR-GENERATOR *provides 100v AC, power of 1,250 watts.*

LP GAS GENERATOR *home model provides 2,500 watts, costs about $550.*

CONVERTER-CHARGER *with power of 500 watts good for emergency.*

CONVERTERS *can be handy during construction or outages.*

of 110-volt power. Its case contains a 12-volt battery and a transistorized converter which changes the battery's 12-volt direct current to a 110-volt alternating current. Two sizes of converter are available with capacities of 250 and 500 watts, costing $150 and $390 without batteries. They will operate lights, or small 110-volt tools or appliances.

To recharge the unit, the process is simply reversed. It is plugged into a 110-volt outlet to recharge its battery.

It has the added advantage that it can recharge car and boat batteries.

The most compact source of power is simply a converter without a battery or recharging circuit. Its cord plugs into the cigarette lighter outlet on the instrument panel of an automobile, and obtains 110-volt alternating current from the car's battery.

The smaller converter shown in the sketches has 42 to 52 watts capacity. It will run an electric razor, or a small radio. The other model shown has 300 watts capacity, enough to operate small power tools. It costs about $175. Other models fall between these two for capacity and cost.

FINANCING AND INSURING CABINS

In cold dollars and cents, financing and insuring a cabin offer no rugged barriers to ownership. But banks and insurance companies look at cabins and residential dwellings in two separate lights. It is worth knowing the rules.

BANK FINANCING

Although banks do not consider vacation property the equal of full-time dwellings as an investment, they will often finance a cabin or beach house.

As a general rule, you will have more success at getting a loan through a bank in the immediate locale of your cabin site than you will if you try to finance a distant retreat with a bank where you live.

The local banker is much more familiar with current conditions and values. Also, any bank is more likely to loan money on a project that is close enough to permit easy and inexpensive inspection and supervision.

You will probably have to make a

big down payment, about 50 per cent. Chances are that interest rates will be the same or slightly higher than you would pay on a permanent residence. The average term for such loans is about 10 years.

If you are unable to get a loan on the construction, you may want to borrow money on other collateral.

Banks usually require that you have firm title to the land on which you propose to build.

Policies and practices of financing vacation construction vary so widely from bank to bank and area to area that you would probably do well to learn the name of a local bank or banks near your property and inquire directly about financing policies. If you are unfamiliar with the area, you can get bank names and addresses from the chamber of commerce.

INSURANCE

Once you have invested heavily of time and money in a vacation place, it is

only logical to give it protection from all the calamities of man and nature.

It is a good idea to consult an insurance company before you start to build. One of their men who is trained in fire engineering can give you valuable and up-to-date advice. Experienced underwriters also can give you an accurate picture of what to expect in the way of coverage for the cabin you have in mind.

If possible, go to the same representative who handles insurance for your house and/or car. If you are a good risk, his company's records will show it, which will improve your chances. Walking in cold on an insurance company which knows nothing about you might result in a turn-down, an understandable attitude since cabins are inherently in unusual danger of snow collapse, falling trees, faulty wiring, lengthy unoccupancy, and unapproved flues.

1. Fire insurance. The basic threat to a cabin or beach house is fire. So the basic insurance policy is fire insurance.

All insurance of this type automatically covers lightning.

Rates are generally low, though they differ from place to place. They are determined by a grading schedule of the National Board of Fire Underwriters, which works with an elaborate system of points of deficiency, depending upon the extent of variance from standards formulated from a study of conditions of more than half a century. In incorporated areas each town is assigned a single rate. If the area is unprotected by an organized fire department, a county rate applies, and it is generally higher than town rates.

Factors affecting these basic rates include: availability and amount of water supply, fire department manpower, size and capacity of department equipment, fire alarm system, police, building laws, strictness of code enforcement, and general geography.

Structure of the individual house has an effect. Construction is taken into consideration. For example, frame construction rates are higher than rates for masonry. Many companies will not sell fire insurance for cabins which do not have continuous masonry foundations.

2. *Extended Coverage Endorsement.* This supplementary coverage may be added to the basic fire insurance at small extra cost. It adds protection against damage from explosions, riots, civil commotion, aircraft, vehicles, and smoke. It also covers windstorm and hail damage on a $50 deductible basis, for a larger premium.

3. *Special Form and Broad Form.* If you wish, you may extend your policy to cover—on a $50 deductible basis—vandalism, malicious mischief, water damage from plumbing and heating systems, glass breakage, falling trees, collapse, ice, snow, and freezing. Special Form provides this insurance for your cabin only. Broad Form covers both cabin and contents.

Cabin or beach house fire insurance, and its two extensions, can be written as endorsements to the fire insurance policy you carry on your regular dwelling. Some of the coverages may be written as a separate policy.

OTHER COVERAGE

Earthquake insurance is available at rather high cost for full coverage. In California there is a mandatory 5 per cent deductible clause. Rates vary only according to the relative susceptibility of the locale to earthquakes.

Theft policies can be written either as a specific endorsement on your basic fire policy, or as a separate policy. If you carry a homeowners' policy on your regular dwelling, it will cover your cabin also, for theft up to $1,000 if the policy is for $10,000 (your cabin must be occupied or in actual use at the time).

If you want or need complete coverage of personal property, you may wish to investigate the personal property floater which can be written to protect all contents of a cabin from practically all hazards including "unknown" risks. Cost of this policy is high.

PERSONAL LIABILITY

If you have a personal liability policy on your home, you can have it endorsed to cover a "secondary" residence for about one-third of the original cost. Liability coverage is particularly desirable if your cabin or beach house is fairly heavily used, and the possibility of injury to non-family members on your property may be high.

SOME TYPICAL COSTS

The cost for fire insurance and extended coverage is comparatively low when you consider the various factors involved. Premiums do vary considerably. A cabin at a remote mountain lake will probably cost considerably more to insure than a similar structure in a densely populated beach colony which has organized fire protection.

As an example of how premiums vary, here are costs for fire and extended coverage for a $5,000 cabin in three widely separated areas of California (assuming in general, unprotected districts): mountain cabin in Tuolumne County, $104; beach cabin at Laguna Beach, $82; desert cabin in Riverside County, $82. All rates are for 1966.

GUARDING AGAINST FIRES

Self-preparedness against fire is vital for cabin owners.

In the country the water supply is often inadequate for fighting fires. Fields of grass and areas covered with brush or timber may add extra fire hazards. Your nearest neighbor may be a mile away. Fire departments, if any, are apt to be even farther away and may be dependent on volunteer help.

If you do live in unincorporated country, these are things you can do to better prepare against fire:

1. Eliminate the chief causes of fires in the home, and around it.

2. Set up some local protection.

3. Establish adequate water supply.

4. Work out a family plan for coping with a fire emergency.

Eliminating Causes

According to the National Board of Fire Underwriters, carelessness with matches and cigarettes is the greatest single cause of home fires. Misuse of electricity is second.

Solutions are simple. Take extra care with the use and storage of matches, especially if children are about. Keep and use generous-sized ash trays for cigarettes. Have an electrician check all electrical circuits, and the loads imposed on them.

Another frequent cause of fires is the improper use of incinerators. There are common sense precautions. Buy an incinerator approved by the local fire department. Place it in the center of a clearing, with at least 10 feet cleared all around. Burn material in it only when lids or doors are closed and the flue is covered by a mesh screen.

Grass fires cause much of the annual fire damage in outlying areas, frequently occurring on the property of absentee owners. New owners should check out county ordinances calculated to eliminate this type of hazard. Individual owners should obey ordinances, and should work with year-around neighbors to assure good compliance.

The most important protective step is to isolate and insulate the building as much as possible from native grass and chaparral that feed fire.

Just as fire departments spend about nine months of the year cutting and clearing fire breaks in Southern California hills, any home owner living in a potentially hazardous area should keep clearing his own fire-resistant break between his house and the brush and grass. This break does not have to be skinned to the ground. Low-growing green plants kept free of dead, dried material are nearly as good as bare earth.

A few plants are notably good in this respect. With regular irrigation, bamboo, eugenia, and even the reputedly combustible pines have performed well.

Where irrigation is difficult, Brazilian and California pepper (Schinus), California laurel, carob, Catalina cherry, lemonade berry (Rhus), and oleander all do well. The better irrigated, the better they do.

Where irrigation is extremely difficult or impossible, four plants show great promise. They are Brewer salt bush, yerba santa, rockroses (especially Cistus purpureus and C. ladaniferus), and sun rose

The break between brush or grass and house should be a minimum of 30 feet in width, though a wider break is advisable.

If you plan to control-burn grasslands on your property, remember that burning grass creates its own draft and will burn uphill. Therefore, start at the top when burning a hillside. Don't start at all unless the area is small enough that you can control the whole area at all times. Don't burn trash in open heaps during the dry season without a permit.

In addition to these precautions, provide room for fire-fighting equipment to get near your cabin and maneuver around it. If the fire fighters can't get safely onto your property to fight a grass or forest fire as it passes, it must wait until the main blast of flames has passed, and this may be too late.

Fire fighters also recommend that you have your street address and name clearly visible at the road. A local chief and his men may know exactly how to get to any house in their district, but when thousands of acres are on fire, other fire fighters and equipment are called in from great distances. They can not be expected to know where

you live unless your address is clearly marked at the road.

Local Protection

The first step in arranging local protection is to find out if your property is under the jurisdiction of any organized fire fighting unit: a county fire department, a volunteer fire department, a special fire district, a state forestry service, or the United States Forest Service.

If you belong to a county fire district or some other separate fire district, get acquainted with the department. Call the station and ask the fire chief or some other official to inspect your property and discuss protection problems with you. Fire chiefs say their own jobs would be simplified if everyone living in the area would do this. It would enable them to learn the exact location of each piece of property, the fastest way to get to it, and to anticipate any special problems they might have in fighting a fire on it.

Forest service fire fighters, federal or state, are primarily concerned with keeping fire from valuable public lands. However, if you are on or next to a state or national forest, it is wise to contact the local ranger, in order to know what help can be expected from the service in case of fire.

If no organized facility exists in your area, it may be possible to organize a special fire district. Here is the usual routine: Fifty or more taxpayers and residents of an unincorporated area petition the county board of supervisors. The supervisors hold a public hearing so protests may be aired. Then they decide if a new fire district should be formed. If so, they fix the boundaries for the new district. Residents of the area elect their own board of commissioners to operate the new service. Funds to pay for organizing and operating the fire district are raised through taxation on the property within the area.

Sometimes a small district can contract with a nearby city or county department for fire protection. Or, if the district operates its own department, expenses can often be minimized by organizing a volunteer group of fire fighters.

Another means of obtaining protection is by petitioning for annexation to an adjoining district that has a fire department. Generally, 51 per cent of the

owners of the property adjoining the existing district are required to be signers of the petition.

The Water Supply

As a rule, water mains in unincorporated areas are seldom adequate for fire fighting. Firemen consider any main smaller than 4 inches in diameter to be merely a supplementary supply. Many country places have only their own water system—a well or springs—which is almost always inadequate in an emergency. A local fire chief or county fire warden can recommend auxiliary water supplies you should have for adequate protection.

If the auxiliary supply is in a tank or pond, be sure that a fire truck can get within 20 feet of it.

Some areas within a fire district have a private water supply serving a comparatively few homes. Such private water companies can profit by cooperative action.

One exemplary group of this type was under the jurisdiction of a fire district, but district funds were insufficient to give the people the protection they wanted. Water pressure in the area was low, and the water mains were only 2 inches in diameter. The members of the coop conferred with fire district officials and a water company adviser.

On recommendation they bought and had installed two used hydrants, and also set up an alarm. Now, when the alarm goes, all families shut off their water to boost pressure so the fire department can use it as a strong supplementary source.

A wise precaution in rural areas where water pressure is adequate for the purpose is to install a rooftop sprinkling system. Pipe and sprinkler heads are of the same type as used in lawns, and are installed in the number the pressure will support. The water company will be able to recommend in this aspect.

Family Fire Plans

Good planning gets people into action quickly, when a fire may be smaller and easier to handle.

Next to the telephone should be posted the fire department number and clear route instructions for reaching your property.

Every person in the family should

know the location of hoses, ladders, buckets, and extinguishers.

Adults should know how to turn off gas and electricity at service entries.

The ladder should be easy to get, easy to handle, and long enough to reach the roof.

Hoses should be connected to faucets at front and back of the building at all times. These should have pressure nozzles. Garden hoses can suffice. But it is better to have a fire hose tapped into the water system at the point with the best pressure. Fire hoses can be bought as kits. Firemen can tell you which size, and where to buy one. The hoses, whatever the type, should reach everywhere inside the house and on the roof.

It is a good idea to have two or three extinguishers in a country place. One in the car or garage, one in the house, and a third in an outbuilding offer good added protection.

There are several types. Some use water, some carbon dioxide, and other kinds use other chemicals. Consult with fire officials before choosing, since each type has a potential weakness against certain kinds of fire.

Have an occasional family conference to rehearse what must be done in the cases of home fires (electric and non-electric) or grass or brush fires.

In the case of brush fires that have too big a head start, there should be an evacuation plan.

Gas and electricity should be turned off at the service entries or meters.

Inflammable outdoor furniture should be moved away from the house, into the open. Canvas awnings should be dismantled.

Close and lock all doors and windows to minimize the chances of fire-fanned winds blowing them open, allowing sparks to get inside the building.

Don't wait too long to evacuate. Heat and lack of oxygen can lead to vapor lock in the automobile. This can leave you stranded, maybe even in the way of the fire equipment.

WAYS TO CLOSE A CABIN

Cabins have to be designed so they can be closed up and left for long periods. Pests have to be kept out. Utilities have to be made safe. Supplies have to be guarded against weather damage.

Weekend cabins especially have supplies of on-hand food in them. These foods need to be tightly sealed to avoid mildew trouble, rodent trouble, or both. The main solution is to keep all foods in tin cans, or canisters with screw tops, if they must be exposed.

Some of the best solutions to rodents have been tin, zinc, or aluminum-lined storage. Where the bulk of supplies is not huge, a cupboard or cabinet will do. Where the supply situation is more complex, it may be easier to line a whole pantry than a series of small cabinets or shelves.

In snow country, leaving liquids on hand can cause all kinds of trouble. Liquids are likely to freeze in cold weather, expanding and bursting their containers.

Cereals and grains ought not be left for long periods in a cabin, because weevils will almost certainly find a way to get at them given any time to work at it.

Bedding has to be stored with as much care as food does. Rodents are very pleased to line their nests with good-quality blankets. Some of the common safeguards against their shredding blankets:

Tying everything in a bundle and supporting it from the rafters.

Lining an enclosed bunk frame with metal and storing all bedding in that space.

Using rodent-proof boxes which can double as storage shelving when the cabin is in use.

The best defenses against rodents, however, begin with the foundation design of the cabin.

Any non-wooden wall will exclude rats, but they can still gain entry from underneath. All a rat needs is a toe hold within 10 inches (its own height) of a free gnawing edge. Sooner or later he will make a hole and gain entry. Usually rats find a toe hold on the foundation, from which they can reach the studding.

The other potential entry in a vacant cabin is through the flues, also a favored way in for birds.

Flues and stovepipes should be tightly capped before any prolonged vacancy. A metal hood or a metal-lined wood hood can be fashioned for a chimney. A two-pound coffee can will fit over a stovepipe, if it isn't hooded to start.

These measures also retard rust in any metal parts inside the chimney.

Dampers should be closed as an added safeguard against rodent entry, and also to keep as much warmth in a cabin as possible. Where there is no damper, a tight plug of paper can help some. Leave a note in the firebox reminding of the paper's presence so it can be removed before instead of after the fire is lit.

Preparing utilities for long idleness is mainly a matter of shutting them all down as far as they will go in cold country.

All pipes should be drained of as much water as possible. Water is turned off at the source. In most cases there is a plug near the turn-off valve. This can be opened to let all residual water drain away. In the absence of a plug, faucets should all be opened.

All U-traps should be dismantled and emptied, the water closet emptied.

Coarse rock salt can be dumped into all pipes to help lower the freezing point of any water remaining.

Electricity can be shut off at the service entry, unless some appliance has to be kept in operation. In this case, or in the case of short absences, all non-working appliances and lamps should be unplugged as a safeguard against either faulty switches or animals gnawing into their wiring, causing short circuits.

The degree to which gas is shut off depends on its type.

Natural gas appliances should be shut down to pilot light operation. Approved appliances now all have safety shut-offs should thermostats fail, or other malfunction occur. Some old appliances without safeties might be shut off entirely.

LP gas appliances should be shut off entirely, and the tank shut off as well. Natural gas is lighter than air, and will dissipate even if an amount escapes into the cabin. LP gas is heavier than air, and will form a pool at floor level as it escapes.

HOW TO BUILD AN ANIMAL-PROOF LOCKER

Here is how to use a sheet metal such as aluminum to make a rodent-proof storage box for food or bedding.

In buying aluminum, get 2-S-soft, .020 thickness if possible. If it is not available, ask for 3-S-soft or utility sheet. The sheets are 24 by 72 inches, usually available from sheet metal shops, lumber yards, or mail order houses.

Substitutes if metal sheets are not available or practical: flattened tin cans or heavy duty window screening.

The main difficulty in lining a box comes with fitting the corners. The best solution is to make a paper pattern.

Using a small piece of paper, fold it into a corner, and crease with a finger tip. With scissors, cut the folds so the paper fits without wrinkling.

The results are transferred to the metal, one corner at a time. The metal is cut so one piece forms the bottom and ends. Two other pieces form the sides.

The bottom piece is cut to lap up one inch on each side, and in one inch from each end.

Trace the pattern on the aluminum. Make short cuts with tin snips. For long cuts, lay a straight-edged object along the line to be cut. Scribe along the straight edge with a sharp pocket knife, hobby knife, or linoleum cutter. Repeat the cut several times. Bend back and forth at the cut until the sheet breaks. The way to hold the sheet still during this operation is with a pair of 2 by 4's sandwiching the metal, and secured by C-clamps. Such cuts will have burrs, and should be filed smooth.

The bending process is similar. Clamp the metal between two pieces of wood, square-edged if possible, with the fold-line about flush with the edge of the wood. Using another piece of wood as shown in the photo, make the bend. This will make a rounded corner. For a square one, make the bend, then hammer the bend square with a mallet.

If the sides are flat, place them after the floor is set. Otherwise, try to minimize exposed joints where fingers are going to be groping later. Secure all aluminum to the walls and floor with nails. Use half-inch galvanized or aluminum nails. Flat-headed, cadmium-plated screws work well also. Secure the metal every four inches.

For appearance's sake, clean the aluminum with a mild detergent to remove grease or finger marks. Follow with a heavy coat of paste wax, or a clear lacquer.

SIDES— 2 REQUIRED

BOTTOM AND ENDS

CUT ON HEAVY LINES
FOLD ON DOTTED LINES

METAL LINING *for a storage locker is formed in three pieces, as the sketch shows. Edges must be covered. 1. Wood blocks clamp pieces for bending. 2. Side patterns should be made after floor is shaped so lap is adequate. 3. Knife cuts are straightest, easier than tin snip cuts. 4. All joints should be tacked at four-inch intervals.*

BUILDING A COUNTRY ROAD

Locating a drive and engineering and supervising its construction are really the province of a professional engineer or landscape architect. This is especially true if your land has tricky slopes, as so much land has in the West.

The Basic Plan

The design, professional or amateur, should follow this basic procedure: On a survey map indicate the rise and fall of the land at certain intervals, and show trees, rocks, and buildings. Then follow the line of least resistance, while observing the safety and practical factors noted below.

Consider placing your drive to one side of your property if possible, leaving just enough room on the property line for a screen planting. This permits a maximum of free space, important on small sites.

There should be nothing to obstruct the driver's vision for at least one car length into the private road. It is wise to keep planting or native plants lower than driver's eye level even farther back.

Along the drive, there should be no planting of trees close enough to bother the driver of the car. Drivers go slower if tree trunks are close to the road. On a long drive, trees close to the edge can keep speed down if that is desirable.

If possible, provide an unrestricted line-of-sight of at least 200 feet at all points along the road.

Roads should curve only when there are solid reasons for their doing so. Some of these solid reasons would include: by-passing a stand of native trees; easing a change in grade by going diagonally across a hill; going around a high spot rather than over or through it, or avoiding extra cutting and filling.

Most of these reinforce the axiom that moving dirt costs money. If you are going on a tight budget, and have a choice, by all means go around or over a high spot rather than through it. It is nearly always cheaper. Bulldozer rates are usually by the hour or day. It is a bargain when the charge is $20 an hour, and it takes a bulldozer an average of five minutes to shove one yard of soft earth out of the way, an average of 15

minutes to clear one yard of rocky soil. The problem of disposal remains after that.

Since either route would be curved (one over, the other around), the general practice is to go around.

Generally it is wiser to traverse a steep slope than to plummet straight down it. However, no road should cross a slide area. Old or new, they are easy to spot. A grown-over old slide is marked by a crescent depression where the slide came from and a hummock where it came to rest.

Also, avoid areas where water is seeping from below ground. Water under a pavement will soon cause it to fail. A tile drain can help—if a professional engineer plans it.

Surface run-off should be prevented from flowing across or onto the road. For a straight road or one with a single curve, a side-of-the-road gutter may do the job. Where there's a switchback, an under-road culvert might be required. Culverts need to be located and designed so water rushing out cannot cause gullying. Baffles at the outlet are one answer. Lined ditches are another, expensive response. An earth ditch is adequate for slopes up to 1½ per cent.

Where the road cuts into a steep bank, particularly a sandy one, sloughing from above is a problem. A diversion ditch high on the slope and a gutter by the road help.

HOW TO PLOT GRADES

Percentage of grade describes steepness. The chart lists those percentages within reason for country roads.

An amateur can do a fairly accurate measurement of a grade with a pair of five-foot stakes, a hand level, some pegs, and an assistant.

A hand level is easy to get, simple to operate. It is a small telescope through which you can sight an object, and simultaneously see a bubble which tells when you are looking along a level line.

There are several ways to measure a grade percentage. The following two seem most accurate for amateurs.

Method 1. To measure an unknown distance from a known rise. Mark one of the five foot stakes at one foot intervals. Sight through the hand level at the five-foot level of the other. Have the assistant move his stake back and forth along the chosen course until the mark

four feet from the ground is level with the hand level. You then have a one-foot rise, and need only to measure the distance between stakes to find the percentage of grade from the chart.

Method 2. To measure an unknown rise from a known distance. Again, one five-foot stake is marked at one-foot intervals. In this case, the assistant plants the stake at a convenient, known distance from the stake with the hand level. Make a level sight, and plot the elevation. Then use the chart to find the percentage.

Once you find well-suited slopes, you can stake out a road course. If it is possible, drive a car or jeep along the course to get the best advance idea of how well it will work. Sometimes it is worth plotting the arcs and angles to make a scale map.

Some deviation will occur when the grading is done, no matter how painstaking the staking. The bulldozer blade will uncover some formerly hidden difficulties.

ROAD DIMENSIONS

The road course has to be eight feet wide as a bare minimum for one-way driving. Fifteen feet is narrow, and 18 feet ample for a two-way road.

An eight-foot road isn't wide enough for anybody to get out of a car, and it does not allow proper right-side vision in the boatier American cars.

A wider road, in addition to easing these difficulties, lasts longer because the wear and tear can be spread over the surface, rather than being concentrated near each edge.

On a slope, what starts out as 12 feet width may narrow to 8 as erosion exacts its annual toll.

A curve must have an inside radius of 28 feet for a car, and 41 for a truck. A full turning circle (on a loop drive) should be at least 60 feet in diameter.

A back-and-fill turn-around area at the garage end of a drive is conveniently sized if it is 25 by 36 feet. That leaves enough room for a guest to park, too.

JOINING THE RIGHT-OF-WAY

Whether your drive enters a county road, a state or federal highway, or a privately-owned tributary road, you have to be sure that grading you do at the intersection does not block drainage alongside the road your drive joins.

FIRST STEP *is grading, best done with large equipment in most cases.*

WATERING *keeps dust down, softens hard spots during the grading.*

RED ROCK *is spread 4 inches thick atop the graded road, then smoothed.*

In most sections of the West, you have to see the county engineer or road commissioner in order to make any change on a county right-of-way. In the cases of state or federal highways, the district highway office or the highway maintenance supervisor is the authority.

These men will tell you what kind of device you should use to cross the right-of-way drain. And they will give some good advice on how to do it.

Where there is a deep ditch, you usually have to run a pipe under the drive fill. Usually, there has to be a stone or concrete headwall around the pipe to prevent its being undermined. The pipe can be of concrete or corrugated metal. The county or state highway official can be of aid in determining the type of pipe, its diameter, and the extent of headwall.

Where the ditch is a shallow one, it may be possible to use what is called a valley gutter to cross the drain. In effect, it is a carefully designed dip in your drive. There are disadvantages, the main one being mud.

GRADING A DRIVE

Grading a road serves to smooth it for use with cars, and provides efficient drainage so the road will stay smooth.

The road must be crowned—graded higher in the middle than on the sides—so water will run off readily. On a dirt-surfaced road, the center line should be higher than the sides at the rate of one-half inch per foot of width (a 9-inch crown for an 18-foot road). For hard-surfaced roads, the rate is one-quarter inch per foot of width (a 4½-inch crown for 18 feet).

Ditches should be installed on both sides to carry off surface water. No great volume of water should be allowed to build up on the higher arc of a curve; it will start to erode the road. A culvert should be installed to shift the burden of the flow to the low side of the road at the point where pressure against the ditch becomes considerable.

Grading and crowning a road by hand tools is folly. A bulldozer or grader can do the job in short time.

The grader, with its movable blade slung underneath, does a good job of grass-roots cutting on fairly level, open land. It isn't efficient in tight places. The bulldozer, its blade in front, costs more, moves more dirt, makes deeper cuts, and is efficient in tough terrain.

In most cases, both machines come into play. The bulldozer roughs out the road. The grader puts the crown on it, and smooths out the rough patches.

Surfacing the Road

Dirt will do on a slight grade, though it will need regular patching under the best of circumstances.

When ruts appear, they can be eliminated by pulling a drag over the road

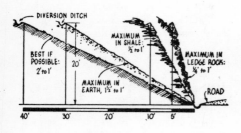

BACK SLOPES *for roads have maximums determined by soils.*

KNOWN-DISTANCE *method of determining a grade with measured stakes.*

KNOWN-ELEVATION *method of determining a grade with measured stakes.*

ROLLER COMPACTS *rock, after which road is usable by automobiles.*

PENETRATING OIL *or other surface is put down to finish road.*

SEVERAL MONTHS *after installation, road is leaf-strewn but smooth.*

behind the car. The drag most used is an adjustable harrow with the spikes set quite flat, and a plank tied on the trailing edge. The spikes roughen the surface. The plank pushes loose dirt into the holes and ruts. To preserve the crown, the drag should be towed up one side of the road, and down the other.

SURFACING WITH GRAVEL

A topping of gravel is the next step up from a plain dirt road. Gravel will bind in with a clayey soil to make a fairly firm surface, enough to keep you from getting stuck in the first mud of the season.

Sharp gravel has the advantage over round or pea gravel that it does lock into place to a degree.

For occasional summer use, a thin gravel blanket of an inch and a half is often enough. For daily use, four inches deep is better.

Stand ready to shovel the loose gravel back onto the road regularly. You will have to.

SURFACING WITH ROCK

If you are going to develop a long-lasting all-year road, your next step after grading is to put in a rock base. Depth varies from four inches over sandy soil to six inches over adobe soil, or in areas that get heavy frosts or snow.

There are three kinds of rock base in common use: 1) a native quarry rock found in most parts of the West, known variously as red rock, rock fill, bank gravel, or rock-and-dirt; 2) river bed or creek run gravel, a natural mixture of aggregates with a silt that acts as a binder; 3) crusher run base, a crushed rock manufactured for use as road base.

Any of these will set up hard and firm when handled right, and if there is not too much clay or soil in the mix. A good rock roadway with no surfacing will last a long time. But pockets will form if the mixture contains too much clay.

A good rock base road can be paved five years later. A poor one has to be ripped up and rerolled before it can be paved.

To make a four-inch base on an 18-foot road, it takes a cubic yard of rock dumped every four and one-half feet along the road. This has to be spread evenly, wet, and rolled. The wetting and rolling sequences usually have to be repeated, and the order of the sequence depends on the composition of the rock.

A dealer usually will have a good idea how to get the best results with the rock he sells.

HARD SURFACES

These commonly used hard surfaces can be put on rock base. The order is from cheapest to most expensive.

Penetration oil. The cheapest of paving surfaces for roads is penetration oil, of which there are four or five grades in regular use. It penetrates and binds a rock base. The surface crust is very slight, just enough to hold down dust.

The oil will not penetrate clay, but can be put directly over other dirt roads.

Many contractors will use this as a temporary paving, to be replaced later by a firmer surface.

Emulsified asphalt. This is asphalt

GRADE PERCENTAGES		
A one-foot rise in	Means grade per cent of	Which, for a road, means . . .
100 feet	1%	Usually minimum for drainage, less would be a problem
50 feet	2%	Gradual grade, not much of a problem
25 feet	4%	Gradual grade, not much of a problem
15 feet	6.6%	Gradual grade, not much of a problem
12 feet	8%	About maximum for high gear at slow speeds in average car
10 feet	10%	A noticeable grade, but easy. Steeper than this, pushing a wheelbarrow is difficult
8 feet	12.5%	No steeper if possible. Can't push wheelbarrow up
6 feet	16.6%	Have to use concrete surface. Brake action downhill and spinning uphill corrugates asphalt
5 feet	20%	Getting into real problems
4 feet or less	25% or more	You really need help. OK for short distances, but safety factor involved. Water rushes down much too fast

mixed with about 40 per cent water. In dry areas, one coat of this on a sandy road will wear very well. It is especially good on volcanic soil. Often it has to be coated with sand or screening so it will not pick up on tires.

Armor coating, or *macadamized asphalt.* Oil is put down over a rock base. Right on top goes a layer of sharp gravel just thick enough to cover the oil. This is then broomed and rolled. Then the process is repeated—usually once, but as many as three times.

The gravel will stick to tires and rattle against fenders for a few weeks, and it may track into the house from a parking area for as many as six months. Some types bleed in hot weather. But once settled down, it is highly durable stuff.

Asphaltic concrete, or "hot mix." Mixed at the plant, it comes hot in a dump truck and is smoothed with a mechanical spreader. It is just short of concrete for durability.

Naturally a deep black, it can be whitened with a cement and water coat.

Cold Mix. It isn't much used as a primary road surface. Rather, it is an efficient patch for any kind of surface.

ROAD COSTS

All the costs of building a road, from grading to paving, vary considerably with distance and accessibility.

As a rough indication, a road 10 feet wide by 500 feet long, fairly near a sizeable town, built in 1966, would cost:

Graded dirt road, $260. Rolled rock, four inches deep, $500. Penetrating oil (¼-gallon per square yard) over rock, $550. Armor coating (2 coats) over rock, $1,000. Asphalt (1½-inch coat) over rock, $1,500.

BUILDING PIERS AND FLOATS

SMALL PIERS *can be tailored to fit the boats they shelter, making it easy to get in or out.*

FLOATS ARE ECONOMICAL *way to extend solid surface out to water deep enough for diving, boat handling.*

A shoreside place on any but open coast is likely to need some kind of pier to fulfill its potential. The need may be moorage for a boat, a take-off for water skiing, a platform for swimmers, or a deck for sun-bathing. Most likely it will be all of those.

A pier, accurately defined, is a permanently fixed platform set over water, resting on pilings driven into the bottom. It can be flexible in design, and is a durable structure. Its disadvantage, especially in tidewater, is that it is not at a constant height above the water.

A float, in contrast, always has its deck a certain height above the surface regardless of tide or other change in level. Floats are not durable, most becoming waterlogged within a few years.

BUILDING A PIER

Structurally, piers are fairly simple affairs. There are only a few general rules to observe in their design.

In tidewater, distance between deck and water at high tide should be 22 inches minimum. In rough water, the distance can be as much as 30 inches to avoid waves washing over the deck, causing rot. In fresh water, 22 inches is a practical distance.

Minimum water depth at the offshore end of a pier should be six feet for safe diving by swimmers. This would be the low tide depth in tidewater. For deep-keeled sailboats, water depth may have to be a minimum of 12 feet.

Dimensions are governed by use. The deck of a pier should be as long as the boat for which it will serve as a moorage. A 12-foot-wide dock allows enough room for a rowboat to be pulled from the water and turned. For swimming, a pier should be wide enough for sunbathers and fully-clothed persons to sit without being doused by the splashes of awkward divers. A versatile design for multiple use is the T.

A pier for moorage should give a boat protection in rough weather. Moorage should be on the lee side, with the bow of the boat headed into the prevailing winds. Pilings can protrude

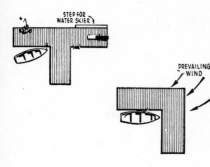

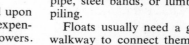

IRREGULAR SHAPES *allow versatile use of a pier or float.*

FLOATS CAN BE SECURED *by any of these three methods.*

WALKWAYS *from shore to main float must be laterally stable.*

through the deck, or cleats can be secured to it for tie-up purposes.

Heavy pilings must be driven by professionals. Piles usually are driven on 12-foot centers, with 6 by 8-inch cross beams between the piles. The beams are capped with 3 by 8's, and the decking is 2-inch lumber.

The perimeter of the pier should be perfectly flush. Anything projecting could tear up a moored boat.

Piling and other timber will last longest if pressure-treated with creosote. Only under pressure is creosote able to penetrate far enough into the wood cells to be really effective. If a piece of previously-treated timber has to be cut, the two ends should be given two coats of creosote which has been heated to a temperature of 150°. Creosote is not used on decking, or elsewhere exposed to clothing or the hides of swimmers.

Untreated piles are often used in fresh water, which does not have the kind of marine life that makes creosote imperative in salt water.

Owners of shorefront on small lakes that freeze over in winter can sometimes build light piers of their own. When the ice is thick enough to bear weight, the amateur pile setter just cuts holes in the desired places, sets light piles, and drives them with a heavy sledge until they won't go any deeper. The system works only with muddy bottom, which will set up around the driven piles. These light piles have to be on shorter centers than heavy ones. Four to six feet is the usual spacing. The beams are correspondingly lighter.

Any pier can be set to one side of the lot to minimize the disruption of the view over the water. Where there are small children, the pier should be in full sight as a matter of safety.

Fencing on a pier is too restrictive to

be of value. Safety fencing is better put on shore, to keep tots off the pier except when adequate supervisors are present.

BUILDING A FLOAT

Float shapes can vary. A float can be square or rectangular, or even U-shaped. The advantage of the U is in mooring a boat. It offers protection to the boat, and lets people debark on either side. The U makes it easy to pitch a canvas tent over the moored boat as protection against sun or rain.

Flotation material will depend upon what is available. It should be inexpensive and have sustained buoying powers. Some proven materials include logs, balsa wood, empty 50-gallon drums, and plastic pontoons.

The best logs are fire-killed cedar snags. They are completely dry and will float high for a long time. Other logs will soak up water until the float is awash after a few years.

Surplus balsa wood rafts, when they are available, also make excellent flotation. The 60-man raft, 12 by 8 feet, and the 25-man raft, 9 by 4½ feet, are the most-used. These rafts are covered with waterproofed canvas, but a coat of tar over that adds to the lifespan and cuts maintenance to an admirable degree.

To make the deck, stringers are bolted together across the top and bottom of the raft, and decking is then laid on top.

Fifty-gallon drums quickly corrode in salt water, or in fresh water if they are immersed the year around. They are not expensive to replace. A summer-only float will last for extra years if it is dragged ashore during the winters. Too many drums make an overly buoyant, unstable float. Some owners float the frame alone, and stuff drums under it a few at a time until the proper buoyancy is achieved.

A foam plastic is impervious to water, and not affected by salt, fungus, dry rot, or marine life. But it dissolves in the presence of gasoline. Pontoons of this material, with a protective coating, can be a good flotation material.

Floats have to be secured in place, but with an allowance for up-and-down movement of tides or seasonal changes in lake levels. It is possible to secure them with a cable and anchor only if they are offshore and free to swing about. Inshore, they can be secured by pipe, steel bands, or lumber around a piling.

Floats usually need a gangplank or walkway to connect them with shore. Few bottoms drop away sharply enough for a float to be secured at the shoreline.

Gangplanks are the typical connection between float and pier. They are ramps connected to the pier by hinges, with the lower end resting on rollers on the deck of the float. Since there is constant motion, the rollers or wheels ought to run on metal tracks or plates, or they will wear through a wood deck in a single season.

Walkways can be on rows of light piles, or can float themselves. Three-foot width is minimal for secure feeling among strollers. Floating walkways need to be made untippable by securing them to alternating pilings, one side and the other. These don't have to be closer together than the length of the log used as flotation.

Pier or float, it is legally necessary to get a permit from the District Engineer, Corps of Army Engineers, before building over navigable waters. The Corps publishes a pamphlet outlining the requirements. The only exception is where a "pier-head" line has been established. In this case, the proposed pier or float has to be cleared by a local authority.

DEVELOPING A WATER SUPPLY

Water on a country place should be clear and free of pollution. Preferably it should also be cool, soft, and free of earthy or other tastes.

To a certain degree, you can treat, filter, and soften water to improve it for domestic use. But you can avoid some of these extra chores if, at the start, you don't buy the place unless it has a source of naturally good water. If local people are satisfied with the water and if it comes from a source apparently safe from pollution, you usually can assume it is all right. Even in this case a water test might surprise you. County health officers sometimes will recommend chlorination of water even though its customary users think highly of it.

Shallow ground water is most likely to be unsafe in populated areas. If a shallow well (next page) appears to be your best water source, and if you have any doubts about the water's purity, check with the county health officer and have the water tested for evidence of bacterial contamination.

Palatable water usually will be safe to use in the garden. But some waters, especially in the Southwest and desert areas, carry considerable minerals or salts that might eventually build up to harmful levels in the soil. If there is a probability of the condition existing on your site, see a county agent or farm advisor.

The Likely Sources

The happiest arrangement is to have your water source—stream, spring, or well—on your own property.

Whenever you bring in water from a neighboring property, buy and have a recorded right to its use and an easement across the neighbor's land for the pipeline.

The present owner may be an old friend. But this protects you against being cut off at some future date should the lands change hands.

Supplemental water can be stored in ponds or cisterns for livestock, irrigation, swimming, fishing, and fire protection. Such water is not generally safe or dependable for domestic use.

STREAM WATER

In the Northwest, and a few other parts of the Western states, there may be an opportunity to obtain safe water from live streams. However, streams are always subject to pollution and muddiness.

In most Western states, property owners along a live stream have a riparian water right. This is the right to take a reasonable quantity of the water for domestic use and for irrigation. Ordinarily, you don't need a permit from a water authority, But in order to take water from a stream that does not touch your property, you have to obtain a water right through purchase of someone else's existing right or by filing application for such a right with the state water authority.

SPRING WATER

A spring is an underground water outflow, usually on the side of a hill. If a spring flows at a usable rate the year around and is located so that it remains safe from pollution, you can often develop and protect it as an economical source of domestic water. However, before you count on a spring, check the safety of its water and the adequacy of its flow. A spring that flows late in the summer of a dry year will probably flow the year around. The best way to find this out is to check with old-timers in the area. If a spring doesn't flow all year, it likely is not worth developing.

The rate of flow from even a good spring is usually too slow for direct piping from spring to house. The answer is to accumulate the spring water in a storage tank that will hold enough to furnish a day's average requirement, or enough to supply water at the maximum rate of use for a few hours. An average person uses about 50 gallons a day for domestic purposes. Garden or other requirements come on top of that. A tank of 500 gallons ought to do for a family of five.

In general, spring development follows these steps:

Excavate and clean spring opening.
Build a wall, box, or dam to catch as much water as possible;
Cover the box bottom with gravel;
Install piping;
Put on a cover;
Install a cattle fence if any of the critters are nearby.

Storage should be organized right along with the spring. Lack of it may lead to the ground around the spring becoming saturated, with the result that water seeps back into the hillside as fast as it is collected.

Variations in type of excavation and design of collection basin will occur with almost every spring. These examples show some basic approaches:

If the water comes out of an opening in rock in an out-of-the-faucet stream, excavation is likely to do more harm than good. The best thing to do is clear away loose rock and dirt from the opening, and make a water-tight box to catch all the water. Cover the bottom of the box with coarse gravel, imbed your pipe in the gravel, and call it quits.

If the spring flow is diffused over a wide area, you should excavate to catch all of this seepage. Sometimes a V-shaped wall with the arms of the "V" extending back into the hill makes the best collecting method for a spring that seeps out over a 10 or 15-foot area.

One of the oldest methods of developing a hillside spring—and one that is still recommended frequently—is to dig a tunnel about six feet high and four feet wide into the hill to a distance of 10 to 20 feet. Dam up the opening of the tunnel with a concrete wall, lodging a pipe through the wall to drain off the flow. Timber the walls of the tunnel, or make a masonry arch, to eliminate the possibility of cave-in. This type very much resembles a dug well that has been laid on its side.

If your tunnel reaches a particularly strong flow of water back in the hillside, it is best to locate the collection basin back in the tunnel. Carry the water from the back of the tunnel to the storage area through concrete sewer pipe or regular water pipe.

A variation is a T-shaped tunnel back into the hill.

Both tunnel systems work best with spring in somewhat porous ground, such as sandstone or limestone. The galleries back into the hillside provide collecting avenues that tap a large part of this porous, water-bearing material.

If a spring flow carries much silt with it, it is best not to imbed your pipe in gravel. The gravel and silt eventually will cement together to close the pipe. Either keep the end of the pipe well above the floor of the spring or catch the silt before it reaches your collection basin by a stepped series of low dams, each with a V-notch.

Where there is evidence of water near the "V" of a draw, a long trench running at right angles to the draw usually will be the most satisfactory development. It should be 15 to 20 feet long, and 6 to 8 feet deep.

The hill should be trenched above the spring to keep out surface run-off and to hold back sliding dirt and rubble. If the spring excavation shows signs of filling with sand and silt, timber the walls or set a box in the hole.

If a spring with a diffuse flow over an area of some 10 or 12 feet occurs on a relatively level spot, you should make an excavation down to fairly solid ground, probably four or five feet deep and approximately in the center of the seepage area. Make a box, without a bottom, the size of the hole you dig. This will hold the water and keep back the soil. You may have to pump your water from such a spring.

Whether you build a box or a concrete dam to collect spring water, take care not to wall off the source.

A slow spring likely as not will get slower if it is dynamited to "open 'er up." The usual result is the cementing shut of the crevices through which water travels.

Spring water can be stored in a small reservoir, an underground cistern, or in a metal or redwood tank. Least expensive is the tank.

Both redwood and metal tanks cost about $80 for a 500-gallon tank. Metal tanks are easier to install if a truck can place them upright on the site. They need to be in shaded places to avoid sun-heated water. Steel needs periodic painting inside and out (unless galvanized).

Redwood has to be kept wet to avoid seepage from shrinking, but will last longer than steel in any situation. Also, it is better insulation against temperature change in stored water.

WATER FROM WELLS

Wells remain the most common source of domestic water for homes in the country. A well is merely a hole in the ground, dug or drilled deep enough to reach below the ground water table. It may be as shallow as 20 feet or deeper than 300 feet. There is ground water in most natural basins and valleys, but, unfortunately, it is not available everywhere.

In the long run, the best source of local water information is always the well driller. He can tell you where wells

have failed and succeeded, how deep they usually have to go in your area, how much they should yield, and how much drilling will cost.

In cases where good water is obtainable a few feet underground, you can dig a shallow well with little special equipment but a lot of labor. The problem is to prevent a cave-in while you are digging. If your soil is a consistent sandy loam, a team of three men can dig about five feet a day. At this rate it would take four days to dig a 20-foot well. Such wells are best lined with concrete pipe. Any well has to be lined or cased to prevent caving in and to keep out dirt and unsafe water. If the lining extends a few inches above ground it will keep out surface dirt and water.

Wells should be covered to protect small children, as well as to prevent contamination.

Because a shallow well is always open to pollution from nearby sewage disposal systems, never locate one within 100 feet of any present or potential septic tank drainage. Deep wells that draw water from gravel strata far below surface are safer as well as more efficient.

Generally, a well is dug only where well drillers are not available. Drillers are usually cheaper. In any case, it is safer to have a well drilled and cased by a professional than it is to do it yourself. An 8-inch drilled well with steel casings costs $3 to $5 a foot. A typical 100-footer costs about $400. A hand-dug well 3 feet wide by 20 feet deep would go about $200.

Where possible locate a well close to the dwelling, so you can use as little service pipe as possible. Cover the well and water system with a small pumphouse to protect the equipment from the weather—particularly from freezing—and sand. A removable roof panel over the well permits you to pull the pump or suction pipe out for service if necessary.

Electric service should go directly to the pump from a central power pole, and not through another building. Thus water will be available if something happens to the building or to the branch circuit in that building.

How Much, How Fast?

Five gallons a minute is about the least flow you can use to meet the needs of a small family home. The smallest water

system sold usually delivers about 4 or 5 gallons per minute, too small to do anything but provide for the household needs of a family of five.

Many experienced pump dealers recommend a system with a larger discharge, if feasible, because they have seen so many people regret not having provided a system to water the garden as well as the family.

In case of fire, the greater water flow available, the better your chance of quelling the flames. Fire underwriters recommend a stream of 10 gallons per minute through a one-quarter inch nozzle, able to continue for two hours. (The total volume would be 600 gallons.)

Some wells and many springs furnish water continuously, but not fast enough. The storage tank described earlier has to go with the slow well.

Many well drillers will pump a new well for a time, to determine its rate of flow. The owner will then know if he has to have a storage tank, and if so, how big.

There are two ways to get pressure into a water system: Gravity, or pump.

A gravity system requires a large storage tank high enough above the water outlets to furnish the required pressure. It takes 2.3 feet of fall to provide 1 pound per square inch of pressure. For 30 pounds of pressure, the bottom of the tank would have to be 69 feet above the hydrant (plus a few feet to compensate for friction in the pipe).

Unless the tank can be located on a hill instead of a tower, the system of pump, motor, tank and tower for a gravity pressure system will cost more than a pure pressure system.

An automatic pressure system is composed of an electric motor, pump, small hydropneumatic tank, pressure switch, and an air volume control. Air under pressure in the top of the tank presses on the water so it will flow out when a faucet is opened. When enough water flows out to reduce pressure to a certain level, the pressure switch turns on the motor which pumps water into the tank until pressure rises again to a point at which the switch turns off the motor.

Most systems are set to turn off at 40 pounds per square inch, but can be set higher if the installation requires it. A moderate size tank is more efficient than a small one since it involves fewer stops and starts, and offers more water in an emergency.

The pump is the heart of the water

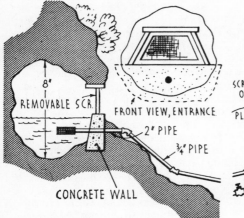

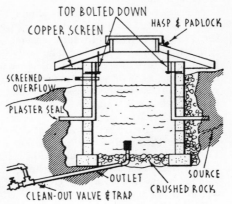

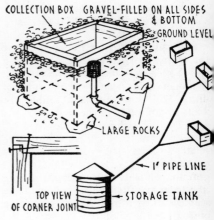

TO COLLECT *diffused flow of spring, cave was dug into hill. Concrete wall dams entrance. Screen covers opening left for cleaning. Caves sometimes are T-shaped.*

EXCAVATED SPRING *is 6 feet deep, 6 feet in diameter. Walls are of concrete blocks, with vertical joints left open. Upper courses sealed with plaster to keep out surface water.*

SMALL SPRINGS *hooked together with 1-inch pipe. Collection boxes are 36 by 27 by 30-inch redwood sunk in gravel. Sometimes, diversion dams have to channel water to boxes.*

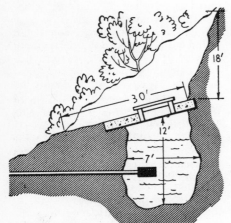

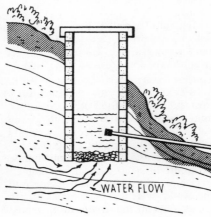

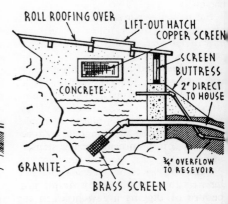

HILLSIDE SPRING *developed by digging a broad collection trench, covering it to protect it from surface contamination. The spring flows a steady 3 gallons per minute.*

THIS SPRING *was once tapped by screened well point. When flow weakened, the hole was dug, 6 feet deep and 2 feet in diameter. Walls are brick. Bottom is gravelled 8-inches deep.*

SPRING OPENING *was simply boxed in with walls of concrete and roofed over to protect a natural collection basin. Such springs flow at highly variable rates, need storage tank.*

system. It lifts the water out of the well and forces it into the tank or service pipe at the pressure required.

A basic factor determining pump size and type is the depth of water in the well. Water can be raised only 22 to 25 feet by suction. A shallow well pump located entirely above ground will suck water up and force it on its way, but a deep well pump is needed to get water

up from 25 feet or deeper. With these, the motor is above ground, but the business end is down in the well, near or in the water.

Of the several types of pump, the jet is now most widely used in domestic wells, deep or shallow. Essentially it is a centrifugal pump aided by a jet or injector. A small stream of water is forced into a venturi tube at the water level,

where it creates a suction. This draws in additional water which is carried up the suction pipe to the rotating impeller. The impeller forces the water on, under pressure, into the tank or supply line. Typically, the motor, centrifugal impeller, and tank are located above the well, with only two pipes extending down the well to the jet.

Choice of pump type and size is best

JET PUMP *and pressure tank are accessible for maintenance.*

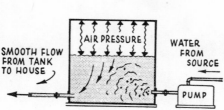

AUTOMATIC PUMP *switches on when pressure drops in storage tank.*

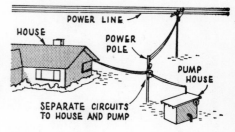

BYPASS HOUSE *with pump circuit, to have water in case of fire.*

left to a dealer, with knowledge of all the technical requirements involved.

Cost of any complete water system will vary widely with the depth and kind of well, and capacity of the system. The minimum cost would be for a shallow, 10-gallon-a-minute well. A total of $275 would be split about $100 for the well

and $175 for a ⅓ horsepower water system. A typical cost for a well would be more like $860, with $360 covering drilling of a 100-footer, and $500 the cost of a 1½ -horsepower system.

In planning, allow $1,000 for water to avoid unpleasant misadventures in the budget.

In areas where several families are building cabins or vacation houses, it is not uncommon for all hands to band together to form a mutual water system. Costs and risks are shared. Individual investment in these ventures is almost always less than would be required in separate action.

PLANNING A SEPTIC FIELD

If you follow expert advice when you install a septic tank system, you take very little gamble on its working efficiently.

Hooking up to a sewer line is always preferable where there is a choice since every septic system eventually must be replaced.

But there is no need for qualms about building beyond the reach of municipal services. The method described here needs only to be accompanied by three very important precautionary steps.

Step one: Test the soil for porosity, preferably before purchasing the site. The test usually is a fairly simple procedure of digging a few holes in the area where the drain field is to go, saturating the holes with water, and then measuring how rapidly additional water will percolate away through the soil. The county health department should supervise. From the specific results and past experience with similar sites in the area, an officer can prescribe the drain field needed.

In many areas, a permit is required to build a private sewage system. The percolation test can prevent complications, since a permit will not be granted where the soil is absolutely impermeable, or where the required drain field would be bigger than the lot. A check of other homes is not enough to convince health officers.

Step Two: To provide an extra margin of capacity, make the system larger than required. In a system with 1,000 square feet of trench floor required, it costs very little extra to expand the square footage to 1,400 or 1,500.

An extra-large tank also adds less to cost than to capacity. For a 1,000 square foot drain field, a tank should be from 808 to 1,080 gallons in size. A 1,500 gallon tank for a few extra dollars will last longer, and will operate much more efficiently.

Some systems have a separate 500-gallon tank for water from the laundry. Detergent in the main tank retards proper bacteria action there—but detergent in the drain field is beneficial because it reduces surface tension of the water.

Step Three: The system, whatever, will need regular maintenance, and, in time, replacement.

You can safely assume that the most adequate drain field will fail eventually. The soil around the sides and bottom of each gravel-filled trench slowly gathers a thin scum that becomes impervious. In good soil, it may be 20 years. In slightly clayey soil, 15 years is closer to it.

The original field should be placed on the lot so that it can be replaced or extended without disturbing anything of importance.

The tank (or tanks if there is a separate one for laundry water) should be placed so they can be reached by the hose from the septic tank cleaner's truck. The tank has to be pumped out every two to five years in most cases.

A reasonably accurate plot plan of the entire system, showing the location of the waste lines, cleanout plugs, tank, and drain field lines, should be made and kept at hand. The plan minimizes the chances of covering the tank with a patio slab or something as immovable. People without plot plans do that sort of thing oftener than county officials care to contemplate.

Some county health departments also file copies of plot plans, along with reports on installations. These can be of service to persons buying an existing cabin.

Septic Tanks

A septic tank is simply a settling tank separating out solids, which remain in the tank. Most are decomposed there by bacteria and eventually become liquid and gas. The remainder settle to the bottom as sludge. The accumulation of sludge and the scum on top of the water are what the septic tank pumper

TWO-COMPARTMENT TANK *is of untreated heart-grade redwood.*

DRAIN FIELD *trenches, 3½ feet deep, are best dug with power.*

TRENCHES BACK-FILLED *with gravel to a depth of a foot, leveled.*

must remove. (It doesn't remove the water from the tank.)

Tanks are made of concrete, redwood, and asphalt-coated steel. Concrete tanks are long-lasting and considered best. Redwood tanks stand up well, are usually lower in cost, and are widely used in the West. Steel tanks are not permitted in some areas because most available models are too small, and rust through on the least failure of the coating.

The shape of a tank—rectangular, round, or oval—makes little or no difference in its efficiency. But a compartmented tank is more efficient than a single-section tank. Usually, the first section is two-thirds of the total volume.

Tests have shown that the average single-section tank dissolves about 60 per cent of the suspended solids, a two-compartment tank about 80 per cent. This is not just a 20 per cent improvement. The double-compartment tank is discharging only half as much suspended matter to clog the drain field.

The size of the tank is important. The small tank will fill up with sludge more rapidly and require pumping out more often. Its smaller capacity also does not allow the dissolving action to go on as long as in a large tank, with the result that more solids are washed on to the drain field.

If your septic tank is located on flat land or elsewhere where rain water can drain into it, the tank needs to be completely watertight. Otherwise, small leaks are permissible. They simply act as additional drain fields, and will clog up in time.

You should have both compartments of your septic tank checked every two years to see if it needs pumping out. A filled tank may back sewage up into the house, and worse, washes sludge into the drain field, clogging it.

Except in cold climates, there is no need for additives or "starters" for a new or pumped out tank. Yeasts often used for the purpose are, in fact, of no value.

There is sometimes an odor from a new or just-pumped tank. It is a sign that not enough of the anaerobic bacteria needed to handle the sewage have appeared in the tank, and other bacteria there are producing offensive gases. The plumbing system vents the septic tank through the house's roof vents, and if a breeze is carrying those gases down from the roof, you notice them. The

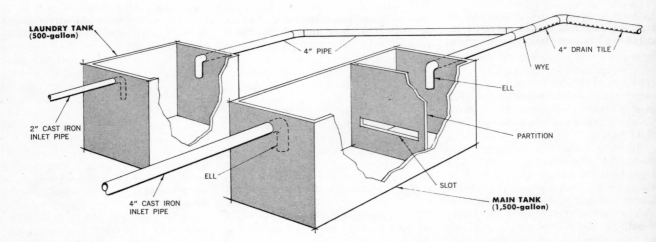

TANKS FUNCTION BEST *if at higher elevation than drain field. Laundry tank optional.*

DRAIN TILE *is laid atop gravel bed. Joints are just slipped together.*

TILE COVERED *with 3 inches of gravel, then asphalt paper goes in.*

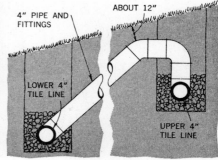

LINES CONNECTED *by device called dam for best flow pattern in field.*

condition usually disappears in a few weeks.

Drain Fields

Though the effluent from a septic tank is further processed by the action of bacteria and air in the drain field, the main function of that field is simply to get rid of the waste water that flows from the house (a daily average of 200 gallons). Most of the water percolates into the earth. Some is transpired by plants into the air.

Two types of drain tile are used: 1-foot lengths of clay tile with pieces of asphalt paper on top of the joints; or 10-foot lengths of perforated bituminous drain field pipe. Both work well. The bituminous pipe can be laid faster.

Whether you use one long or several short lines, and how they are laid out in a pattern, are details that vary somewhat with each site, with final decision up to your health department or builder. The field should never be located in a low, non-draining depression. Even if dry and absorbent at the time of building, that soil will probably be saturated in wet weather, and then your drain field will flood and fail.

Storm drains should never be piped into your septic system. They will flood it in wet weather.

Your drain field may consist of one or more gravel-filled trenches, or it can be a 10-foot or wider seepage bed scooped out by a bulldozer and back-filled with gravel with the drain tile laid around its perimeter. This latter type is usually less expensive on level ground and it can fit into a fairly small space, but it works well only if the ground underneath is quite porous.

The functions of the gravel fill are to keep soil from clogging the drain tile holes and allow the waste water to reach as much of the trench's bottom and side soil surfaces as possible.

Tile lines need to be approximately level, so the waste water will spread evenly throughout the field. On hillsides, this means the lines follow contours.

Where there are two or more lines of tile on a hillside, "dams" are particularly important. These dams are raised sections of the 4-inch pipe connecting lines of drain tile that are at different levels. An example is shown in the drawing above.

A dam forces the effluent to seep out first into the upper line, rather than all flowing to the lower. The normal daily flow of effluent stays in the uppermost line of drain tile. Within a few years the soil around it becomes clogged, and then all the effluent passes over the dam or dams into lower lines of tile. But it continues to go first into the uppermost line, which acts as an additional septic or settling tank, with the result that the lower lines of tile perform much longer before becoming clogged.

Distribution boxes formerly served the purpose of dams, but are no longer recommended by the U. S. Public Health Service because they needed cleaning oftener than they commonly got it.

If your field fails, the symptoms will be quite obvious: a raised local water table, surface seepage, backing up of sewage into the house, or odor nuisances.

If there is room, you can extend the drain field of a defective system to increase its capacity.

If a test hole reveals suitable soil at deeper levels, sump holes or seepage pits are often used to increase the capacity. These are either holes drilled with power augers and filled with gravel or larger porous-sided wells. Their use should be checked with your local health department, because these seepage pits can sometimes pollute underground waters.

Wait until after a heavy rain and let the dirt fill settle in the ditches before planting a lawn over a new drain field. That first rain sometimes floods a new field, but less storm water will enter the system after the disturbed soil has compacted.

There is some controversy as to the advisability of raising large plants or trees over your drain field. Some experts believe that the deep roots penetrate and plug the drain tile. The U. S. Public Health Service in a survey found very few cases in which roots had actually entered the tile. Seeking water, the roots found it in the gravel fill and soil outside the tile (because water is continually draining out and down from the tile instead of being carried inside it as it is in a sewer line). Thus plant roots seem to stay outside, and, of course, they do increase the permeability of the surrounding soil. Large plants also draw in and evaporate considerable amounts of the water, though not in wet weather when this would be the most helpful.

Where an automatic washer is in use, the drain field should be oversize, because a washer uses about 45 gallons of water per load.

PHOTOGRAPHERS

Jerry A. Anson: 87 (top left, bottom right), 90 (top left, right), 120 (left). William Aplin: 52, 53. Architectural Photographers: 36, 37. Ray Atkeson: 6. Morley Baer: 15, 16, 17, 40, 41, 59 (top right), 76, 91 (top), 92 (top right, center), 98 (bottom left), 99 (top right). Nancy Bannick: 46. John Bickel: 68, 69. Bernice Blundon: 94 (right). Brant Studio: 120 (top right). Ernest Braun: 8, 9, 10, 11, 24 (bottom), 32, 33, 38, 39, 43, 58, 59 (top left, bottom), 86 (bottom), 95 (bottom right), 98 (top left). Tom Burns Jr.: 48, 49, 65, 67, 92 (bottom left), 97 (bottom right). Carroll C. Calkins: 98 (bottom right). Clyde Childress: 19. Glenn Christiansen: 20, 21, 22, 23, 94 (left), 96 (left), 97 (left, top right), 99. Maarten Claringbould: 75, 84. Bob Cox: 27. Richard Dawson: 12, 13, 14, 26. Dearborn-Massar: 92 (top left), 95 (bottom left). Philip Fein: 98 (top right), 115. L. O. Gocean: 100. Mike Hayden: 30. Art Hupy: 45, 64, 95 (top left), 96 (right). George Knight: 54, 55. Edmund Y. Lee: 85. Philip Molten: 18. Don Normark: 47, 56, 57, 62, 63. Phil Palmer: 31. Maynard Parker: 92 (bottom right), 93 (center right), 95 (top right). Arnold Paulson: 62 (bottom right). Charles Pearson: 34, 35, 42, 44, 89, 90 (bottom), 91 (bottom), 93 (top left), 95 (center left, lower middle). Hugh Stratford: 4. Julius Sherman: 29 (bottom). Darrow M. Watt: 60, 78, 79, 125, 126. R. Wenkam: 61, 86 (top), 93 (top right). The color photograph on the cover is by Ernest Braun.